# Mindfulness

How to Use Mindfulness and Meditation and
Create a Calmer Mind and More Peaceful Life

(Simple Practices to Empower Yourself and
Transform Your Life)

**Gregory Lakin**

Published by Rob Miles

© **Gregory Lakin**

All Rights Reserved

*Mindfulness: How to Use Mindfulness and Meditation and Create a Calmer Mind and More Peaceful Life (Simple Practices to Empower Yourself and Transform Your Life)*

ISBN 978-1-989990-82-7

All rights reserved. No part of this guide may be reproduced in any form without permission in writing from the publisher except in the case of brief quotations embodied in critical articles or reviews.

Legal & Disclaimer

The information contained in this book is not designed to replace or take the place of any form of medicine or professional medical advice. The information in this book has been provided for educational and entertainment purposes only.

The information contained in this book has been compiled from sources deemed reliable, and it is accurate to the best of the Author's knowledge; however, the Author cannot guarantee its accuracy and validity and cannot be held liable for any errors or omissions. Changes are periodically made to this book. You must consult your doctor or get professional medical advice before using any of the suggested remedies, techniques, or information in this book.

Upon using the information contained in this book, you agree to hold harmless the Author from and against any damages, costs, and expenses, including any legal fees potentially resulting from the application of any of the information provided by this guide. This disclaimer applies to any damages or injury caused by the use and application, whether directly or indirectly, of any advice or information presented, whether for breach of contract, tort, negligence, personal injury, criminal intent, or under any other cause of action.

You agree to accept all risks of using the information presented inside this book. You need to consult a professional medical practitioner in order to ensure you are both able and healthy enough to participate in this program.

# Table of Contents

INTRODUCTION .................................................................. 1

CHAPTER 1: HOW TO BEGIN YOUR MINDFUL MEDITATION PRACTICE .................................................................... 3

CHAPTER 2: HOW TO BREATHE MINDFULLY ..................... 22

CHAPTER 3: MINDFULNESS IN DAILY LIFE ......................... 28

CHAPTER 4: FLOW STATE ................................................. 34

CHAPTER 5: MINDFULNESS: DO IT YOUR OWN WAY! ...... 44

CHAPTER 6: HOW TO USE COGNITIVE RESTRUCTURING IN THE REAL WORLD ............................................................ 52

CHAPTER 7: RELIEVING STRESS THROUGH MINDFUL YOGA .................................................................................... 62

CHAPTER 8: PRACTICAL HABITS ....................................... 69

CHAPTER 9: MINDFULNESS & MEDITATION .................... 87

CHAPTER 10: MINDFULNESS AND THE PRESENT MOMENT .................................................................................... 93

CHAPTER 11: LEARNING TO MEDITATE .......................... 102

CHAPTER 12: BUILDING YOUR SELF-CONFIDENCE .......... 111

**CHAPTER 13: MINDFULNESS EXERCISES FOR STRESS, PAIN AND SUCCESS** .................................................. 116

**CHAPTER 14: LETTING GO** ............................................... 132

**CHAPTER 15: MINDFULNESS AT WORK** .......................... 140

**CHAPTER 16: MINDFULNESS TO ELIMINATE STRESS** ...... 150

**CHAPTER 17: INCREASE YOUR CHANCES OF SUCCESS** .... 153

**CHAPTER 18: THIS IS YOUR BRAIN ON STRESS** ............... 156

**CHAPTER 19: MINDFULNESS THINKING** ......................... 163

**CHAPTER 20: 30 SIMPLE MINDFUL TECHNIQUES YOU CAN PRACTICE ANYTIME** ....................................................... 168

**CHAPTER 21: APPLYING MINDFULNESS MEDITATION DAILY** ................................................................................ 187

**CONCLUSION** ................................................................. 190

## Introduction

What is Mindfulness? It is the essential human capacity to be totally present, aware of what we are doing as well as where we are. Mindfulness is something that everyone possesses. However, it is something that requires practice to nurture the abilities.

In this book, you will learn all the techniques needed to find your mindfulness and how to practice it daily as well as the fundamentals of why this practice can help you to manage stress, relationships, work and create an overall better you.

In this book, we will discuss first what stress is, how it affects your mind and body, and how to manage it. We will then go through the first steps of Mindfulness and what is required as you begin training your mind. You will learn what your narrative is, how to be non-judgmental, how to curb greed, liberate yourself from suffering, and how to rid yourself of the delusions of self-fulfilling prophecies.

Lastly, after we have discussed how to allow your mind to start processing all of that clutter, we will learn techniques you can use to practice mindfulness daily. Techniques for mindfulness in breathing, mindfulness in eating, mindfulness in emotions and thought, and mindfulness of sounds. All this awaits you, so let's begin.

## Chapter 1: How To Begin Your Mindful Meditation Practice

If you want to create a regular practice of meditation, you need to first prepare yourself, your schedule, and your space. You prepare yourself by making a commitment to the practice and sharing your commitment with others so you have a sense of accountability.

You want to be in a positive state of mind, open to all outcomes and possibilities without preconceived judgments or desires, simply knowing the benefits of meditation will reveal themselves in time. However, remember the purpose of these early sessions is to train and quiet your mind, so enter the meditation understanding this as the goal.

Determine the time a day when you will meditate, and choose a time in which you can eventually work up to thirty minutes of meditation. But in the beginning, start with just five or ten minutes and increase your time slowly. You might try a meditation in the morning and one in the evening if possible.

Find a space in your home that is peaceful and conducive to meditating. You might want to light some candles, dim the lights, and remove any distractions or possible noises. Let others in the house know you are meditating, and ask them not to disturb you.

Here are the basic steps for a mindful meditation practice:

**1. Sit comfortably either in chair** or cross-legged on the floor with a cushion. Keep your spine erect and your hands resting gently in your lap. Don't recline as you may fall asleep. Erect posture will help you stay alert and awake.

**2. Close your eyes,** or keep them open with a downward focused gaze, then take a few deep cleansing breaths—maybe three or four.

**3. Notice your body** and the feeling of your body touching the chair or the floor. Be aware of your body in the space around you.

**4. Gradually become aware of your breathing.** Notice the air moving in and out through your nostrils and the rise and fall of your chest and abdomen. Allow your breaths to come naturally without forcing them.

**5. Allow your attention to rest** in the sensation of breathing, perhaps even mentally thinking the word "in" as you inhale and "out" as you exhale.

**6. Every time your thoughts wander** (which they will do a lot in the beginning), gently let them go and return to the sensation of breathing. Don't judge yourself or your intrusive thoughts. Just lead your mind back to focused attention on breathing.

**7. As you focus on breathing,** you'll likely notice other perceptions and sensations like sounds, physical discomfort, emotions, etc. Simply notice these as they arise in your awareness, and then gently return to the sensation of breathing.

**8. When you observe you've been lost in thought,** detach yourself from the thoughts and view them as though you are an outside witness with no judgment or emotion. Label them by saying, "There are those intrusive thoughts again." Then again, return your attention to the breathing.

Continue with these steps until you are increasingly just a witness of all sounds, sensations, emotions, and thoughts as they arise and pass away.

Taming the Monkey Mind

In the beginning, you'll find you must redirect your thoughts almost constantly. You will often get caught up in the past and future and feel frustrated with your inability to tame your thoughts.

But with time and practice, it will become easier and easier to just be the witness to all thoughts and sensations and remain focused in the now. You will experience immense peace in shedding attachments to everything except the present moment.

When you are outside of meditation in normal life, you carry many burdens and stresses in the form of thoughts. It's like having an albatross around your neck you must drag with you everywhere you go.

During <u>meditation</u>, you give yourself permission to remove the albatross and abandon the burdens. This creates the right attitude for freedom and joy in your meditation. As you begin your meditation, remind yourself to release and banish the past and future.

This means you don't think about your worries, your work or family, your childhood, or anything in your recent history. During meditation, you become a blank slate with no past or future and no interest in the past or future.

I love the description Theravada Buddhist monk Ajahn Brahm uses on his website to teach students how to manage unwanted thoughts:

"I describe this as developing your mind like a padded cell! When any experience, perception or thought hits the wall of the 'padded cell', it does not bounce back again. It just sinks into the padding and stops right there. Thus we do not allow the past to echo in our consciousness, certainly not the past of yesterday and all that time before, because we are developing the mind inclined to letting go, giving away and unburdening."

During meditation, it is common to anticipate and worry about the process of meditating or the possible outcome you will or won't reach. You also may fret over how long the meditation will take or the small pains or discomforts you're feeling.

During the early days of meditating, you'll wonder if the effort is really worth it. You might think, "Nothing is happening here. This is a waste of time. I don't see the purpose of this." You will feel your mind is a wild monkey that can't be tamed. You might even have a moment of stillness of mind, and in your excitement start a commentary on the experience—which removes you from the present moment.

Rather than engaging in commentary with every thought or feeling, simply observe and direct your attention to whatever is happening in the moment. Then observe whatever comes up and go back to the moment, and so on over and over. If you redirect your attention to the moment after every observation, you don't have time to get lost in commentary. It is like redirecting a toddler back to his bed until he gets the message you mean it.

Even if you don't feel like you're making progress, you are. Just keep at it. Acknowledge that millions of practitioners can't be wrong about the rewards of meditation and stay committed, knowing you will improve.

Just as you work for several weeks in your job before you get your paycheck, you must put in the time in meditation before you get the payoff. At some point, you will abide in silent awareness long enough to experience how sweet and blissful it is.

BENEFITS OF MINDFULNESS

The term "mindfulness" has been used to refer to a psychological state of awareness, the practices that promote this awareness, a mode of processing information and a character trait. To be consistent with most of the research reviewed in this article, we define mindfulness as a moment-to-moment awareness of one's experience without judgment. In this sense, mindfulness is a state and not a trait. While it might be promoted by certain practices or activities, such as meditation, it is not equivalent to or synonymous with them.

Several disciplines and practices can cultivate mindfulness, such as yoga, tai chi and qigong, but most of the literature has focused on mindfulness that is developed through mindfulness meditation — those self-regulation practices that focus on training attention and awareness in order to bring mental processes under greater voluntary control and thereby foster general mental well-being and development and/or specific capacities such as calmness, clarity and concentration.

Researchers theorize that mindfulness meditation promotes metacognitive awareness, decreases rumination via disengagement from perseverative cognitive activities and enhances attentional capacities through gains in working memory. These cognitive gains, in turn, contribute to effective emotion-regulation strategies.

More specifically, research on mindfulness has identified these benefits:

**Reduced rumination.** Several studies have shown that mindfulness reduces rumination. In one study, for example, Chambers et al. (2008) asked 20 novice meditators to participate in a 10-day intensive mindfulness meditation retreat. After the retreat, the meditation group had significantly higher self-reported mindfulness and a decreased negative affect compared with a control group. They also experienced fewer depressive symptoms and less rumination. In addition, the meditators had significantly better working memory capacity and were better able to sustain attention during a performance task compared with the control group.

**Stress reduction.** Many studies show that practicing mindfulness reduces stress. In 2010, Hoffman et al. conducted a meta-analysis of 39 studies that explored the use of mindfulness-based stress reduction and mindfulness-based cognitive therapy. The researchers concluded that mindfulness-based therapy may be useful in altering affective and cognitive processes that underlie multiple clinical issues.

Those findings are consistent with evidence that mindfulness meditation increases positive affect and decreases anxiety and negative affect. In one study, participants randomly assigned to an eight-week mindfulness-based stress reduction group were compared with controls on self-reported measures of depression, anxiety and psychopathology, and on neural reactivity as measured by fMRI after watching sad films. The researchers found that the participants who experienced mindfulness-based stress reduction had significantly less anxiety, depression and somatic distress compared with the control group. In addition, the fMRI data indicated that the mindfulness group had less neural reactivity when they were exposed to the films than the control group, and they displayed distinctly different neural responses while watching the films than they did before their mindfulness training. These findings suggest that mindfulness meditation shifts people's ability to use emotion regulation strategies in a way that enables them to experience emotion selectively, and that the emotions they experience may be processed differently in the brain.

**Boosts to working memory.** Improvements to working memory appear to be another benefit of mindfulness, research finds. A 2010 study., for example, documented the benefits of mindfulness meditation among a military group who participated in an eight-week mindfulness training, a nonmeditating military group and a group of nonmeditating civilians. Both military groups were in a highly stressful period before deployment. The researchers found that the nonmeditating military group had decreased working memory capacity over time, whereas working memory capacity among nonmeditating civilians was stable across time. Within the meditating military group, however, working memory capacity increased with meditation practice. In addition, meditation practice was directly related to self-reported positive affect and inversely related to self-reported negative affect.

**Focus.** Another study examined how mindfulness meditation affected participants' ability to focus attention and suppress distracting information. The researchers compared a group of experienced mindfulness meditators with a control group that had no meditation experience. They found that the meditation group had significantly better performance on all measures of attention and had higher self-reported mindfulness. Mindfulness meditation practice and self-reported mindfulness were correlated directly with cognitive flexibility and attentional functioning (Moore and Malinowski, 2009).

**Less emotional reactivity.** Research also supports the notion that mindfulness meditation decreases emotional reactivity. In a study of people who had anywhere from one month to 29 years of mindfulness meditation practice, researchers found that mindfulness meditation practice helped people disengage from emotionally upsetting pictures and enabled them to focus better on a cognitive task as compared with people who saw the pictures but did not meditate.

**More cognitive flexibility.** Another line of research suggests that in addition to helping people become less reactive, mindfulness meditation may also give them greater cognitive flexibility. One study found that people who practice mindfulness meditation appear to develop the skill of self-observation, which neurologically disengages the automatic pathways that were created by prior learning and enables present-moment input to be integrated in a new way. Meditation also activates the brain region associated with more adaptive responses to stressful or negative situations.

Activation of this region corresponds with faster recovery to baseline after being negatively provoked.

**Relationship satisfaction.** Several studies find that a person's ability to be mindful can help predict relationship satisfaction — the ability to respond well to relationship stress and the skill in communicating one's emotions to a partner. Empirical evidence suggests that mindfulness protects against the emotionally stressful effects of relationship conflict, is positively associated with the ability to express oneself in various social situations and predicts relationship satisfaction.

The effects of meditation on therapists and therapist trainees

While many studies have been conducted on the benefits of applying mindfulness approaches to psychotherapy clients, research on the effects of mindfulness on psychotherapists is just beginning to emerge. Specifically, research has identified these benefits for psychotherapists who practice mindfulness meditation:

**Empathy**. Several studies suggest that mindfulness promotes empathy. One study, for example, looked at premedical and medical students who participated in an eight-week mindfulness-based stress reduction training. It found that the mindfulness group had significantly higher self-reported empathy than a control group. In 2006, a qualitative study of therapists who were experienced meditators found that they believed that mindfulness meditation helped develop empathy toward clients (Aiken, 2006). Along similar lines, Wang (2007) found that therapists who were experienced mindfulness meditators scored higher on measures of self-reported empathy than therapists who did not meditate.

**Compassion.** Mindfulness-based stress reduction training has also been found to enhance self-compassion among health-care professionals (Shapiro, Bishop, & Cordova, 2005) and therapist trainees. In 2009, Kingsbury investigated the role of self-compassion in relation to mindfulness. Two components of mindfulness — nonjudging and nonreacting — were strongly correlated with self-compassion, as were two dimensions of empathy — taking on others' perspectives (i.e., perspective taking) and reacting to others' affective experiences with discomfort. Self-compassion fully mediated the relationship between perspective taking and mindfulness.

**Counseling skills.** Empirical literature demonstrates that including mindfulness interventions in psychotherapy training may help therapists develop skills that make them more effective. In a four-year qualitative study, for example, counseling students who took a 15-week course that included mindfulness meditation reported that mindfulness practice enabled them to be more attentive to the therapy process, more comfortable with silence, and more attuned with themselves and clients. Counselors in training who have participated in similar mindfulness-based interventions have reported significant increases in self-awareness, insights about their professional identity (Birnbaum, 2008) and overall wellness.

**Decreased stress and anxiety.** Research found that premedical and medical students reported less anxiety and depressive symptoms after participating in an eight-week mindfulness-based stress reduction training compared with a waiting list control group (Shapiro et al., 1998). The control group evidenced similar gains after exposure to mindfulness-based stress reduction training. Similarly, following such training, therapist trainees have reported decreased stress, rumination and negative affect (Shapiro et al., 2007). In addition, when compared with a control group, mindfulness-based stress reduction training has been shown to decrease total mood disturbance, including stress, anxiety and fatigue in medical.

**Better quality of life.** Using qualitative and quantitative measures, nursing students reported better quality of life and a significant decrease in negative psychological symptoms following exposure to mindfulness-based stress reduction training (Bruce, Young, Turner, Vander Wal, & Linden, 2002). Evidence from a study of counselor trainees exposed to interpersonal mindfulness training suggests that such interventions can foster emotional intelligence and social connectedness, and reduce stress and anxiety (Cohen & Miller, 2009).

Similarly, in a study of Chinese college students, those students who were randomly assigned to participate in a mindfulness meditation intervention had lower depression and anxiety, as well as less fatigue, anger and stress-related cortisol compared to a control group (Tang et al., 2007). These same students had greater attention, self-regulation and immune reactivity. Another study assessed changes in symptoms of depression, anxiety and post-traumatic stress disorder among New Orleans mental health workers following an eight-week meditation intervention that began 10 weeks after Hurricane Katrina. Although changes in depression symptoms were not found, PTSD and anxiety symptoms significantly decreased after the intervention. The findings suggest that meditation may serve a buffering role for mental health workers in the wake of a disaster.

**Chapter 2: How To Breathe Mindfully**

Breathing mindfully can be practiced either sitting or standing, and can be done no matter where you are. The only thing you need to focus on is being still and paying attention to your breathing. You can begin by slowly breathing, allowing your inhalations to pass through the nose and come out through the mouth. Your breath should come into and out of your body without effort. You should be able to allow all of your thoughts to rest for the time being. Forget about the tasks you need to accomplish in the day and let yourself stay still for now.

Paying Attention to your Breath:

You should learn to pay attention to the breath on purpose, noticing the air as it goes into the body and nourishes you, and then noticing it as it leaves you and enters the world again. You might not be a person that expects to like meditating, but if you can do this, you are already on your way. Let's take this a step further.

How Long does it Take to do this?

The recommended time for getting into the habit of mindful breathing is 15 minutes a day. You might find it helpful to increase this number as you go to receive maximum benefits.

Actionable Steps for Mindful Breathing:

Find the Right Time: Putting aside a specific time of day to do this is best, but you should avoid doing it when you are especially anxious or stressed out. Experts have said that doing this regularly can help you deal with hard times more effectively.

Get the Right Posture: You can pay attention to your breath either sitting or standing up, but being in comfortable posture is ideal. You can keep your eyes closed or open as you see fit, but closing your eyes might help you focus better. Many people find that sitting up straight helps their mind stay alert and focused.

Stay Relaxed: Pay attention to your body and let it completely relax. Notice if there are any particular spots in the body that feel tense or stressed, and consciously allow them to calm down and relax. You should feel completely at ease now and relaxed.

Focus in: The first step to breathing mindfully is to pay attention to what your breath is doing, including all of your inhalations and exhalations.

Breathe: When you first begin this, particularly during stressful times that call for calming, you can start by breathing very deeply, in an exaggerated way. Breathe deeply through the nose for at least 4 seconds, and then hold it for 2, then exhale for 5 seconds. You can start to observe your breath as you breathe, and make sure you aren't trying to judge or alter it in any way. Instead, focus on the way your chest moves and the way your breath feels as it enters and exits your body.

Notice the Mind: As you breathe, you might notice that your mind keeps wandering, thinking about sensations in the body and your mental happenings. This is perfectly fine and natural. Your only job here is to notice it and calmly call your focus back.

The Essence of the Breath in Mindfulness:

Pay complete attention to what your breath is doing, feeling its natural progression and flow. It goes in, it goes out. There is nothing here that needs to be worried about or fretted over. In fact, you don't even have to make any effort for this natural process to happen. Your breath should not be too long or too short, simply allow it to happen as it wishes to happen. Try to breathe into your entire body, instead of simply your lungs.

Noticing the Space between Breaths:

When you breathe in and out, there is a very subtle and hardly perceptible pause of space that happens. Pay attention to the moment of pause, in between your breaths, in order to become fully present. When you start to do this, your mind might begin to go crazy and wander, and you may find that you begin thinking of other stuff at this time. When this does occur, there is no issue here, and it's completely natural and expected to happen. Your only job here is to notice when it occurs. To yourself, you can calmly say, in your mind, "wandering", and then pull your focus back to your breath.

Ideally, you should stay within that space for up to seven full minutes at a time. Pay attention to the breath, in a completely calm and silent moment. Every so often, your mind will get distracted, but you simply need to call it back to the task at hand. A couple minutes will pass by, then you should notice the body again, the entire body, sitting here it is. Allow your body to relax even deeper, and then give yourself a moment of appreciation for what you are doing.

**Chapter 3: Mindfulness In Daily Life**

As mentioned in the first chapter, to attain peace and to relieve yourself of unnecessary stress, mindfulness must be applied in your daily life. The state of mind you enter during meditation should be continued when you go about your day.

Of course, this is difficult and almost impossible. Being mindful around irritating co-workers or between angry honks of traffic will take considerable effort. But that's why you are encouraged to extend the practice during these situations. Don't simply wait for meditation to bear its fruits. Work on it.

Below are a few pieces of advice and tips to help you get through daily situations:

**1.** When eating.

It's common now to update social media sites, check emails, watch TV, and chat with whoever you're having dinner with while eating. Modern life's fast-paced setting demands it, but this is the reason why many people forget to appreciate the explosion of flavors every bite holds.

To truly relieve yourself of stress, put your phone away, turn the TV off, close your laptop, and ask the other person to save your conversation for later. Instead, pour all your awareness on the food, at your every move, on the table, and the people sitting beside you. Again, thoughts and judgments will inevitably come. When they do, recognize them but let go before you have the chance to grip and embrace the emotions that it comes with. This is what it means to be in the present -- to be mindful.

**2.** During conversations.

Remember that conversation you saved for later? This gives the other person the impression that you are giving him or her lesser value, but it's actually the opposite. Before, it was common courtesy to pay attention to the person you are conversing with, and this means stopping whatever you are doing to actually listen. Today, however, conversations (and significant ones) mostly happen over lunch or dinner, while watching TV, as you both scroll on your tablet or phone before going to bed, or during long drives. How much percentage of what has been told had actually been heard?

In the workplace, despite placing communication on top of the list of office mantras, how well does each employee really do understand each other? Everyone pays attention during conversations, but more likely than not, the mind is actually venturing between one horrible thought to another. Some examples are, "This girl must have been wasting all her time putting that thick make-up on that's why the report wasn't finished on time," or "My boss is an idiot who knows nothing of how difficult this job is," or simply, "Just get the work done! I don't need and want your excuses!"

Sincere communications happen under the light of mindfulness. Again, never judge the person, or give meaning to his or her words. Accept them as they are. And in the workplace, instead of completely restricting the conversation within the bounds of work, add a little sympathy. Before nicely demanding for pending work, ask your co-worker how he has been doing and how has he been coping with heavy loads work. These little greetings not only develops kindness in the workplace, it can lead you to the root cause of problems in the company (should there be any).

**3.** During commutes.

A stressful day at work can make anyone feel cranky, leaving reality even more irritating. And this is why the commute back home is everyone's most hated part of the day. The stink of the underground tubes is unbearable, and the buzzing crowd and tight spaces is enough to annoy the hell out of anyone. The only defence you have against reality is an imaginary escape to the beautiful beaches of Fiji, or the solemn songs of Adele.

Practicing mindfulness during this hopeless situation seems impossible. Besides, Buddha, the monks, and everyone else who came up with the practice had likely never experienced exhausting commutes before. Well, the second statement may be right, but being mindful during these travels isn't impossible. Don't focus too much on what you feel on everything that's bothering you. Instead, think of other people. All of them could be just like you -- rushing to get home to their families, and thinking of how beautiful life would be if they were in the Bahamas.

Daily life presents several other situations where you need to practice mindfulness -- during showers, while cooking, in long queues, when brushing your teeth, and more. But basically, how to deal with them is all the same. Turn your awareness from your emotions and thoughts, and into reality.

## Chapter 4: Flow State

The great part is, after a little bit of meditation practice, once you're able to quiet down your thoughts, you can get into what is typically referred to as the "flow state" fairly easily and consistently.

I want to talk about conditioning for a bit. If you think about it, everything you currently do, from what you eat to your exercising habits to your beliefs are all due to past conditioning. Literally everything you do is the result of past actions and circumstances. An in-depth conversation about this will have to wait till the next volume, but I want to leave you with one simple idea. If you take this as true (even if you don't believe it, just try it on for a minute), what that means is your future is nothing more than the result of the conditioning you're doing now. It is a little more complicated than that, but it can be a useful way to think about your experience. Why would you do anything now that wouldn't condition you favorably later on down the road? If you think about it like that, you have a better chance of eating better, taking better care of yourself, engaging in supportive rather than negative self-thought and so on.

This is not some New-Agey Law of Attraction kind of thinking. This is simply observing the way the world works. Everything seems to work due to cause and effect. Right now everything you're doing is the effect of past causes. But it also means that the future is at the effect of past causes and right now will soon become part of those causes.

All these things are in the future. You're where you are at now simply because of past conditioning, circumstances. With this in mind, you can now start to affect that conditioning. That's an incredible key to life. Condition now for what you want later.

Easier said than done, right? What do you do when you know what conditioning you should be doing, but you fall for the most immediate thing? The easy thing. After all, being able to do deep practice and focus on what you really want is the key to success in anything. So, let's say you know you should be doing something, like exercising, but you really feel like laying on the couch watching TV instead.

Here's the trick. First, use what you already know. When in doubt, note it out. In case you haven't figured out already, you can use the noting technique at any time, not just when you're sitting or walking. So if you're experiencing resistance towards doing the right thing, they probably start with thoughts in your head. Note them thinking, thinking, thinking.

Then you may find yourself feeling something in your chest. In these situations, it almost feels like a physical pull. I start to imagine what it feels like to be sprawled out on the couch relaxing. I can imagine exactly how good it will feel to lay down and do nothing. Hard to do anything else at that point? Nope. I just note the feeling – feeling, feeling, feeling. More thoughts might bubble up – "I'll just wake up early and exercise." Thinking, thinking, thinking.

I will also note any other senses that are contributing. Seeing, hearing, touch. I will start noting fairly quickly trying to monitor my entire experience as closely as possible. By doing this for just a little bit, maybe a few minutes, you'll be able to burn away those sensory desire feelings. You'll know immediately how you're doing - you should start to feel clear with less clingy-type thoughts. If not, keep noting.

Now there's one more thing. If the thing you're noting has a particularly strong pull and you can't keep track of all the sensations that make it up, feel free to start with the big sensation of wanting. In this case, I would note wanting, wanting, wanting. Keep noting that way until it breaks back into smaller sensory experience you can track. I know previously in this book, I mentioned that it's always best to track at the sensory level and drop any judgments of the sensory experience (like anger), but in this case it seems to help. You see that the wanting is just a sensation. Maybe when you first notice it, it's a pretty big sensation combined with thought but it's all tangled up. Just focusing on it will help. Allow the experience to take you where it wants, but I can almost guarantee if you stick with it long enough, it will break down to smaller sensations and thoughts that you will have an easier time managing.

Here's the deal, at the end of this, once you feel concentrated, have some sensory clarity of the experience and feel like you have equanimity, you may still decide to crash on the couch. But at least the decision will not have been made at the whim of some body sensations that arose.

You have a better chance of making a clear, rational decision.

If you do decide to the couch option and watch TV, you can still use this time to practice mindfulness. Whenever I first sit down to watch TV, I always place my awareness on the body sensations that make up breathing. Rising, falling. Rising, falling. Maybe in between breaths I will note seeing, seeing, seeing.

Since watching a movie or TV requires some aspect of mental processing, you won't be able to note the entire time. But if you feel you're losing focus, just place your mind on the breath again for a few reps. If you've been practicing the Sitting Meditation, your mind will quickly go back to this concentrated state. That's just more conditioning at work.

Although at this point in my practice I can lose the words, I still do use them as placeholders when I'm doing something that requires little processing power. If I'm just walking from my car to a store, I will note the steps, mostly out of habit. I use the words still, because I know how addicted I am to thought and how easy it is to fall off the wagon and back into the downward spiral of constant narrative thinking.

There are 3 different ways you can structure your practice. This part is highly inspired by the work of Shinzen Young, who first came up with these practicing modalities.

First is duration. Pretty simple concept. You simply practice meditating for longer and longer. The goal is to stay with the object of concentration for a little bit longer each time. This builds patience and overall skill.

There are 2 components to duration. How long can you meditate in one sitting? What is the longest meditation session you've ever had? Can you go for 3 or maybe 4 hours? You can build up your concentration muscle (and back muscles) by doing long-haul mediation sessions and gradually building up longer and longer sessions over time. The great thing about this is, the more you concentrate, the more you concentrate. It's something that builds on itself. By increasing your ability to concentrate for longer periods of time, you will also increase your concentration in other areas of your life.

Ok, the next way to practice is called trigger practice. This is when you expose yourself to triggers that may impact your performance or concentration. Shinzen talks about using this for meditation by putting something on TV that typically elicits a strong emotional reaction from you. You note your experience until you get concentration, sensory clarity and equanimity. Being able to carry this skill out into the world where there are emotional triggers everywhere is what it's all about, so practice exposure to various stimulus to train yourself to keep cool and calm.

The last form of practice is motion practice. This is fairly straightforward (and in some ways overlaps with trigger practice and even walking meditation). Practice being mindful while standing up. Practice while walking. Practice it while lying down. Practice while running. Practice it while a passenger in the car. You want to be able to keep your concentration, sensory clarity and equanimity while in movement.

Duration, trigger and motion practice can and should all be used in your formal meditation practice. Occasionally, try to go for a sitting session that's longer than what you've previously done. If you usually do an hour, try a two hour session from time to time. After you've built up some concentration muscle, you can try for even longer. Practice noting when listening to an opposing political view that makes your blood boil. The goal isn't to change your beliefs, but rather to greet all experience with concentration, clarity and equanimity. Once you get good at sitting and walking meditation, try to do it lying down. Then try to do it while exercising. I love to do some noting in the morning when I'm stretching and doing a few yoga poses (check out the 5 Rites for pretty easy and quick but powerful exercises you can do every day). Adapt the noting you use during the walking meditation or use whatever words feel natural to you.

And lastly, any time you feel any kind of emotional overwhelm or thought overwhelm, don't be afraid to note it out. You may not be able to eliminate all unpleasant emotions or thoughts, but it doesn't hurt to try. You may be surprised at how often you can quickly get relief with this technique.

It's enough talking for now. If you haven't already, spend at least 20 minutes using one of the 3 practice techniques. With very little narrative thought in your head, you will likely have the experience many call "becoming one" with your experience.

You may no longer notice a separation between yourself and your doing. This is very good! If you aren't quite experiencing that yet, don't worry. We'll talk all about that in the next book. When you're done practicing, come back and we'll talk about what to do next.

**Chapter 5: Mindfulness: Do It Your Own Way!**

We have given you a list of some easy, simple but definitely effective techniques for you to try and get your concentration and focus back into your life. Does that mean you have to follow what we've written word by word, and practice them until you get used to them?
Not really, no!
Don't just sit back and listen to what this eBook tells you. Do your own invention, and make up your own rules and

techniques. Make up some meditation and mindfulness routines that suit you better.

Each one of us is different with different realities and different sets of problems. We have different levels of concentration and need different stimulations to force us to focus.

Instead of only following the techniques mentioned in this book, take the general idea from it, and make up your own rule. If you are satisfied with the idea of mini and one-minute mindfulness techniques as mentioned in the previous chapter, then use them in your daily life. Choose the options of sound, object, touch or meditation to concentrate better.

If you would rather perform meditation-based techniques once or twice a day, then take the tips from the techniques above and design your own exercise routines to fit your surroundings, your environment, your lifestyle or your choices.

Be vocal in what you are looking for? Are you looking for a quick-fix to improve your concentration one dreary afternoon before an important presentation? Are you looking to gradually improve your concentration power and focus so that you are more susceptible to everything that is happening around you? Do you want a complete change in your ability to look at life? Are you looking forward to not miss a single moment of everything that life has to offer you?

Know yourself – that's the key!

Shut the door, switch off the mobile, and keep the laptop off for the moment. Switch off the light, and take a comfortable seat.

Take a deep breath, focus your thoughts, and now ask yourself –

- Have you ever looked at that curtain that has been hanging on your widow for months? Can you remember exactly what they look like? Can you draw the designs on a piece of paper without looking at it once?

- Have you asked your neighbor this morning how she is doing? When was the last time you have talked to her? When was the last time you invited her over for coffee? Can you remember what she last told you about her granddaughter?

- Can you make a list of the things you have done just yesterday? Do you remember what you ate for breakfast? How did you prepare your egg? What was the flavor of the sandwich you ate for lunch yesterday? Did you drink a cola with it, or a coffee?

- What was the last thing your partner/spouse told you before they left for work? Can you remember what they were saying about their latest project at work? Did you remember what you replied to their description of their office party?

Surprisingly, many people don't remember the answer to most of these questions. This is because when we are living a busy life, many things that happen near us, to us or for us, pass on without us even acknowledging it.

Our mind works automatically most of the time. When our neighbor is telling us a story about their grandchildren's latest escapade, we are busy in our own mind thinking of what to cook for dinner. When our partner is telling us about their work, we are thinking of our own projects. We may listen to the words and even manage a few 'aha!' and 'definitely's, but we barely remember the details later.

This is what happens to the best of us, and the most of us. This is nothing to be ashamed about, but it is something, definitely, to work on. And the first thing that you need to do is to start thinking.

Don't let life pass you while you are only concentrating on the supposedly bigger things in life - a.k.a. the promise of a promotion in the future, an exam, the mortgage or diabetes. Instead, concentrate on the smaller things that eventually go by when you are too busy. Don't miss the rainfalls in worrying about getting wet. Rather, concentrate on how the water is falling about you. Don't just listen to a song because you need to pass your time in the subway. Listen to what the song is trying to say, listen to how the tune is trying to make you feel inside.

Forget what impact it has on you 10 years later or even tomorrow. Has it made you happy just for the moment? Has it made you feel better as a human being? Do you feel in harmony with the world in this very moment?

Stop worrying for a moment about what you are going to cook for dinner when you get home. Listen to the sound of the traffic outside, or look at a beautiful flower when you are passing the florists. Concentrate on the simpler, smaller things, and the biggest thing of all - life - will seem brand new to you!

Don't make any judgments. Don't think whether your life is good or bad. Don't stress yourself too much. Go with the flow and be comfortable with who you are. Concentrate on what's around you, focus on the life that you are living at that very moment.

Imagine yourself as a traveler who has no worries, no obligations! It's when you are free that you are most powerful, when you can do anything. You are a hitch hiker who is going to take on the beautiful things of the foreign land that you are visiting. You have no boundaries, no time limits to do that in. You are not a visitor who have spent a lot of money in travelling to a foreign country and must therefore, force yourself to have fun. You have to see everything of that country because you have spent money to go to it - that should not be your attitude.

Take in as much of this world as you can. Be ambitious, but don't forget to concentrate on the smaller things.

Just be in the moment!

But we are not asking you to stray yourself from your loved ones! Mindfulness has a lot to do with how you feel about yourself and your relation you're your surroundings - it may be your parents, it may be your spouse/partner, it may be your pet and it may be that orchid plant hanging down your glass window. This is an art of attachment with them while at the same time having the impression to make yourself feel.

What's holding you back? Nothing, except yourself!

You are the person who's holding you back. It's how you think that's holding you back. Let go of all the worries and you will find a peace within yourself which you have not thought possible.

## Chapter 6: How To Use Cognitive Restructuring In The Real World

So now you know how to use mindfulness and you know how to use cognitive restructuring. Hopefully you've also been able to guess how the two might be linked: we use mindfulness in order to identify the negative thoughts and then we apply cognitive restructuring in order to change them.

This has been used for a while now in order to treat things like phobias, anxiety disorders, addictions and much more.

But what if you don't have any of those problems and you're completely 'fine'? Well in that case… we can still use cognitive restructuring. Because the thing is, you can actually use cognitive restructuring to improve aspects of your thought process that aren't 'broken'. In other words, this isn't just a tool for healing but also a tool for self-improvement. And there are countless ways you can use it to make yourself calmer, more confident and more productive.

Likewise, there are many things that are similar to cognitive restructuring but don't technically fall under the same heading.

We'll be returning to this concept more in future but for now, let's look at some alternative ways to control your thought patterns and some alternative motivations for doing it.

Fear Setting

Often we think of fear and anxiety as being short term responses to situations or stimuli. But in fact, our fear and anxiety can be much longer term and affect our decision making, goal setting and decisions.

Tim Ferriss proposes a concept called 'fear setting' in his book The Four Hour Workweek as a tool you can use to overcome your fears and thereby start getting what you want out of life. Let's say you're thinking of starting a new job, taking a career break so you can go travelling, or starting your own business. You've been thinking of doing these things for a long while but the problem is that you're too afraid to do it because you think you'll that you'll end up without a job or without a partner. Surely if you leave your current job to go travelling, you won't be able to get a job on your return? And the longer you're unemployed, the more unemployable you'll become. Eventually your partner will become sick and tired of scraping by because of a stupid decision you made and they'll leave you. Then your house will be repossessed. And then you'll end up homeless and alone.

That might all sound very over-the-top but this is the kind of thing we actually think on an unconscious level all the time. And the reason we think it is that humans are naturally very risk averse. We evolved in the wild where 'risk' would generally mean 'lions'. As such, we learned to become more sensitive to risk and to defend our assets more than we go after new assets.

But today risk is very rarely anything life threatening. More likely, risk will mean 'getting shouted at' but we blow it out of proportion because we're risk averse people.

By now, you should hopefully be able to guess what's coming next: thought challenging. We're going to take these beliefs and fears and challenge them by looking at just how realistic they are.

And Tim Ferriss' technique is perfect for this.

So first, think about what it is you want to do and why you want to do it. Now think about all the things that are right now holding you back from taking the plunge and giving it a go. If we're talking about taking a career break, then your list of fears and reasons might look like so:

Now's not a good time, you don't have much money

You don't want to leave your partner for that long
You're afraid your job won't be there when you get back
You're afraid you won't be able to find subsequent employment
You're afraid that you might ultimately end up destitute, in debt or homeless
Now let's assess each of these beliefs. To do that, we're looking not only at how likely they are but also how you'd cope if it were to happen. Think of contingencies and things you can do to prevent them from being likely.
Now's not a good time, you don't have much money
There's never actually a good time – and if you travel smart you don't need much money
You can work online while you travel
You actually won't need that much money
Now is probably better than later
You don't want to leave your partner for that long

They probably don't mind

If it's important to you, then it's something you have to do

It's preferable to feeling resentful toward your partner because they prevented you from seeing the world

You're afraid your job won't be there when you get back

It probably will be – discuss with your employer

Do you love your job that much?

You're afraid you won't be able to find subsequent employment

This is highly unlikely – if you're skilled then travel will simply add to your CV

You could even find a new job and agree to start later on

If necessary, then you can take a part time job or start a side business to tide yourself over

You're afraid that you might ultimately end up destitute, in debt or homeless

You can live on savings a long time

You can earn money in other ways

You probably have parents or friends who would take you in long before you went homeless

Now think about the alternative: do you want to never go travelling? Do you want to spend every single day stuck in that office without ever accomplishing the things you want to accomplish? Let this motivate you more than the fear and now make the decision to take the plunge.

The same technique can help you to make the decision to start a new career, to move country, or to do all the countless other things that you've been dreaming of doing.

Remove the Fear and Date Anyone

So in this case we've used thought challenging again to break down our fears so that we can go after whatever we want in life.

But another method you can use is to acknowledge those fears as real but just find a strategy that minimizes the risk. In this section, we'll look at a technique you can use this to do in dating that will give you the confidence to approach and date everyone.

So let's say that you're the average awkward guy, for argument's sake. You go to bars regularly with friends hoping to 'pull' but you're too afraid to approach the people on the dance floor. Why? Because you're worried they'll reject you and you'll thus end up feeling incredibly awkward. That's a genuine concern (although we could ask why it matters) so it's hard to deny it out of hand.

The simple solution? Minimize the risk and remove your likelihood of failing.

To do this, you can simply assess the situation before you approach anyone. So hang back away from the bar and chat with friends. As you do, just look around the place for people you're interested in and if you see someone, smile and them while making eye contact. If they're interested, then you can bet they're going to smile back. If they're absolutely not interested? They'll probably just look away and you'll know about it. But in either situation, you haven't lost face and you can still hold your head high. There's nothing to be afraid of.

If they've smiled though, then you can probably relatively safely approach them. That doesn't mean they're necessarily into you but it means they at least are open to the idea of chatting with you. So the next step is to head over in your group of friends to talk to their group of friends. Don't speak to them only; speak to the whole group so you simply come across as someone friendly, outgoing and interesting. Likewise, let your friends mingle with their friends too. When you get a moment, try to spend a bit more time chatting with the person you were initially interested in and who gave you the go-ahead to come over.

If conversation is going well with the person you're interested in, then you can step it up one more notch by simply offering to buy them a drink. This is a very clear signal that you're interested in them and so they probably won't say yes unless they're interested back. Now they're away, you can talk to them on their own and assess the situation.

Finally, ask if they want to dance. And if they say yes, take the same approach: dance more and more closely until eventually you're completely sure it's okay to make the move.

In this situation, you have now approached someone attractive in a bar but at no point is there any danger of rejection. If they don't want to talk to you, they won't smile. If they aren't interested when you come over, they'll make excuses and you can talk to their friends. If they change their minds, they can say no to the drink. If you're giving off the wrong signals, then they can say no to the dance. But at no point have you embarrassed yourself and you haven't done anything that you can't 'bounce back' from.

Think about other things that you're afraid to do in your life, assess why it is you're afraid, and then think of ways you can get around that fear by avoiding the worst case scenarios!

## Chapter 7: Relieving Stress Through Mindful Yoga

Mindful yoga was first developed as a therapy for individuals suffering from Posttraumatic Stress Disorder (PTSD). This practice transforms movement and yoga into a form of mindfulness meditation. Combining awareness and hatha yoga cultivates greater mindfulness. Mindful yoga focuses on mind/body awareness rather than the "perfect" posture. Yoga postures promote relaxation and calmness provides a stress-relieving effect. Combing mindfulness with yoga can significantly reduce your stress level. Apart from reducing stress, mindful yoga offers other benefits including improving lung capacity, increasing flexibility, improving the brain function and increasing the sense of balance. People who regularly practice mindful yoga experience improved quality of life.

Mindful Yoga Postures

To practice mindful yoga you'll need an uncluttered place with a flat surface. Remove all distractions from the practice area. Practice in bare feet. Clothing should be loose but not too loose. Avoid pushing yourself beyond your limit.

To get the maximum benefits, it is recommended to practice regularly. Do your postures on a completely empty stomach. However if you feel hungry, you may eat some light snacks and wait for a while. If thirsty, drink some water.

If you take your yoga practice outdoors, avoid crowded places and direct sunlight. Although no instrument is necessary, you can use some (i.e. yoga block, yoga ball) if you like. Use a mat (ideally yoga-mat) to avoid slipping and sliding. Breathe naturally and remember not to hold your breath while going through the postures.

When you're ready, bring your attention away from any external distractions and tap into how you feel. Allow yourself to let go of any goals you have for practice (e.g. feeling stress-free or being more mindful). Allow the practice to unfold on its own, and let go of any particular attachment to how it should manifest itself. Let us start with mountain pose:

Mountain pose (Tadasana)

Mountain pose is the foundation of all standing yoga postures. You can find elements of this pose in all asanas.

To practice this posture, stand with your feet together or slightly apart. While standing, make sure, your weight is evenly distributed on both feet, and your chin is parallel to the floor. Feel the shinbones draw into the mid-line of the body and the thighs internally rotate towards the back.

Move your head slightly to align with the center of your pelvis.

Notice if the flow of your breathing is natural— check if it's rhythmic and consistent.

Press your feet into the floor. Focus on the contact points of the toes and the heels. Become aware of all the sensations that arise— the warmth or coolness in the contact points of your feet, the subtle swaying of your body and the flow of your breath.

As you're breathing in, lift your chin and raise your hands from the sides with palms facing each other. Stretch your arms and reach your fingers towards the sky. Push your pelvis slightly forward. Exhale.

Close your eyes and stay in this posture for a while. Become mindful of the sensations that arise from the stress points. Slowly lower your hands and open your eyes. Be conscious of the movement of the body every time you transition between postures.

Thunderbolt Pose (Vajrasana)

From standing posture, kneel on your shins. Make sure thighs are perpendicular to the floor and the soles of your feet have positioned either side of your sacrum. If you're having difficulty sitting in this posture, use a folded blanket or yoga block to sit on.

Place your hands on your thighs. Keep your head straight and lengthen from your tailbone all the way through the crown of your head.

Close your eyes, breath naturally. Feel the contact points of your body with the floor. Become aware of the sensations that arise from those points. Open your eyes. Switch to the next posture.

The Cow-Cat Pose

From the thunderbolt posture, ground the hands into the floor and bring your thighs in a position perpendicular to the floor with your knees and toes touching the ground.

Your body is in a 'table-top' position now. As you breathe in, draw your chest forward and upward, broadening the collarbones as the shoulders draw down the back and lift your chin up. Become aware of the stretch points and the sensations arising from those points. This is Cow pose.

As you breathe-out, lower your head while arching the upper and middle spine, so that it looks like a cat stretching out.

Become aware of the stretch points and sensations that arise from those points. This is Cat pose.

Again breathe in, draw your chest forward (cow pose) and breathe out and round-up your torso (cow pose). Practice those postures back and forth a few more times while being aware of the sensations of your breath and the stretch points.

Slowly rise up from the floor, and enjoy your new-found, stress-free state of mind.

## Chapter 8: Practical Habits

A List of Simple Mindful Habits for Everyday Living

Mindful practice is beneficial to our everyday living and can help us to attain sustaining inner peace. It will also help you to be in a loving accord with everybody around. Mindfulness habits will enable you to have a better insight into your sense of purpose and placement in life. You will also be able to empathize with your shortcomings and the shortcomings of other people.

These habits are as follows:

Learn how to be grateful

Taking note of all the good things that life is blessing us with is a vital mindful habit which we should practice daily. When you are grateful for the blessings you are enjoying, you will find out that there is something that you need to be thankful for even when you are at your darkest moment.

Focus on one specific habit

It is important to note that this practice is a gradual process. You should only take one beneficial habit at a time, to begin with. When you continually follow this positive habit in your everyday living, it will become second nature to you. You will become accustomed to it and start living the habit spontaneously.

Practice feeling your palms and feet

One of the evidence of physical self-awareness is when you can bring yourself to the present. When you tightly clench your palms and release it or clench your toes and release it, it is a sure way to become aware of the present moment.

Be aware of your environment

Gradually take note of your surroundings without having to manipulate your reactions or feelings. Make yourself aware of what is going on around you. Instead of trying to remain standstill in the present, move on. Although it may not be an easy task, you can achieve it if you try. You can take a stroll in a park, nature-endowed areas or by the sea. As you walk, free your mind from thoughts and take note of the enticing aroma, objects, sounds and activities around you. Allow yourself to become a spectator of the environment and try not to judge the presence or purpose.

Set a continual alarm

When you have an alarm that will ring at the pre-set time to alert you to awareness, you will be saved from operating on autopilot. The alert will serve as a reminder for you to leave every other thing you are doing or thinking to focus objectively on your feelings and thoughts.

Take a deep breath

Taking a deep breath and letting it out slowly increases your life-span according to Yoga teachings. Breathe in and gently count to three, you can then breathe out and do it again. As you feel the fresh and oxygenated blood rushing inside your body, your life will become renewed.

Make this practice a priority

The practice of mindfulness needs prioritizing for it to be effective. You need to be very close or on top of your mental knowledge and taking on the duty of a gatekeeper for your everyday tasks.

Reduce the noise

Try to switch off your electronic gadgets like tablet, TV, and Smartphone for some time. If you become used to the quietness, you will soon discover that you do not miss their noise and they too, gradually, will not miss you.

Do not hear only but listen too.

For you to carry out a conversation with another person, it needs your time and undivided attention. It is a special privilege if you can listen attentively and communicate with other people. When you are mindful of this privilege, it means that your undivided attention is involved for the entire time. It also means that you are present mentally for the duration of the interaction.

Be mindful of what you eat

You should be mindful of what you eat and do not involve yourself in other activities while eating. Sniff, look and taste the food you want to eat. If you follow mindfulness practice in the things you eat, it will trigger your ability to pinpoint the food that your body relies on naturally. It can also help you to identify the foods that are for quick relief and convenience. As you are eating, contemplate the entire food process starting from when it was planted till when it ended up on your table

Wash out the cobwebs

Taking a shower to clear out the cobwebs is tested and proven to be effective in mindfulness practice. When you wash away the unnecessary thoughts or limiting factors, you will come out fresh, renewed and ready for flourishing.

Do away with the computer and mobile apps that waste your time.

Any mobile or computer application that you did not use for one month means that

that particular app is not essential. Therefore, do not clog your life with unnecessary applications that will waste your time and effort as you are browsing through what you require.

Make reading a habit

Cultivating the habit of reading is another form of mindfulness practice and the appropriate way to focus your mind at home. As you are reading, it brings the same effects as when you are meditating. Your thought pattern will slow down calming your mind, and your heart rate will reduce thereby increasing your ability to concentrate.

Sub-divide your day in parts

This practice of subdividing your day will help you to become aware of the way you are spending your days. It will also help you progress naturally to becoming mindful of the way you will spend the rest of your life.

Practice meditation or queue up

Make out time to meditate, but when it is not possible due to a shortage of time, you can select a very long queue and join it. The time you are waiting for your turn makes you aware of your placement at that moment.

Napping

Sleeping for half an hour or a few minutes is the best way to "be" for some time.

Always smile

It is important to always smile to all because you do not know who will be in a position to offer you help in the future.

Pay attention to your instincts

If you are practicing mindfulness, as time goes on you will become connected to your intuition and be able to trust its directives. With mindful practice, you can enhance your inner guide. That particular voice that many people often ignore because it is always contradicting your logic is the way that leads to inner peace. Begin to trust and listen to your intuition and see the positive result for yourself.

Select your words

You should be careful of the way you speak to others. Do not talk to them with a misguided belief or preconceptions which may not entirely reflect our innermost personality. Our feeling of anger, personal frustration, fears, and insecurities help to shape your tongue and word pattern. You should not fall into autopilot way of speaking with a harsh tone instead, speak kindly without being judgmental or critical.

Be kind to yourself

Make time to take note of the way you are speaking to yourself. Speak kindly to yourself as you are kind to others. You should be patient and praise yourself. Learn how to cheer for yourself on your efforts since it is the best way to combat the challenges of life. Again, you should learn how to forgive your shortcomings.

Learn how to cry

When you cry, you are connecting to your physical reactions, feelings, and thoughts. Crying is like exposing your weakness and an excellent way to release your pent-up emotions. Crying will rejuvenate your soul and allows you to live in the present moment.

Step by Step Guides for Living a Mindful Life

There are practical, simple ways that you can live a mindful life and invite positivity into your life. You will be surprised to view your life every day with more clarity, joy, purpose, satisfaction and more fulfillment. Mindfulness practice is noiseless, yet it is strong enough to change the way we view and live our lives. It will not only help us to live more at the moment, but it can also transform our reactions to stress, our behavior, the way we feel, the way we view our feelings and how we communicate with our loved ones. Here are some step by step guides for living a mindfulness life:

Engage yourself in hobbies that are meaningful

When you include meaningful hobbies to your mindfulness practices, your life will become more enjoyable, with fulfillment and richness. Hobbies like reading books will give you time to relax, forget your worries or thoughts and live in the present. If you find that your mind is wandering, and you are reading a page without understanding it, you can re-focus your mind so that you can go back to reading and be in the present. Cooking is another hobby that will help you to focus and remain in the present.

Another important hobby that you need to practice with mindfulness practice is Yoga. Practicing Yoga is another way to unwind and be in tune with your body. It allows you to take notice of your feelings, breathing and this action compliment mindfulness practice. It will also strengthen you to face the challenges and stress of your everyday living.

Use your everyday tasks as an opportunity to practice mindfulness

If you are in the habit of making use of your daily chores to practice mindfulness, you will not feel pressured, and your life will become more meaningful. Keeping your environment clean every day is a great way to add more meaning to your life. As you are cleaning, be attentive to the movements of your hands and how they feel.

Although their movements may be reflexes which you overlooked, you can utilize their actions by paying attention to them mindfully. Another crucial hobby that promotes mindfulness practice is washing plates. When you are washing dishes, be mindful of the sensations you can feel. You should take note of the scent of the dishwashing soap, the slippery nature of the plates, the warmth of the water and the smooth surfaces of the dishes.

Agree with anything that stimulates you to be happy

Always agreeing to things that light you up is a favorable choice which enhances mindfulness practices. You do not need to only say yes to what you think is necessary instead say yes to anything that brings you joy even if they are not essential. To always agree with the things that light you up to do not mean that you have to spend money on buying new things for yourself. You can agree to things like self-care, trying new things, goals, experiences and spending quality time being with your loved ones.

Making room for positivity

Creating room for positive things in your life is helpful to practice mindfulness. For instance, taking time out for meditation, relaxation, movement and for mindfulness without feeling pressured that time is being wasted with these frivolous activities.

If it's not possible to create the space at home, you can always find a place that you can go to have your space. It may be places like a garden café, your backyard, your village, a park, workshop, the beach, a lake, the gym, a meditation class, your car or any event center. This is the perfect way to eliminate all the bad feelings clustering your life and recharging yourself with positivity.

Going to these places will provide you with the feeling of safety, calmness, and comfort in your time of distress or sorrow.

Integrate happy habits to your daily living
Inculcating habits that make you happy is the perfect way to bring positivity and mindfulness to your everyday living. Having your habit means that you only add to your life whatever you want or choose to do and how many times they occur.

If you have the habit of reading one novel each week or monthly, write a journal weekly or drinking chocolate instead of coffee, it is entirely up to you. Since it is your habit, you can choose to increase or decrease the rate at which you go about it. However, if you find out that the habit wants to enslave or stress you out and prevent positivity and mindfulness, you can always eliminate the habit.

If the elimination solution does not make you happy, you can always make room for flexibility so that it can be easier for you. Habit is something that you do not allow to operate on autopilot. If you do so, you may not notice your mind wandering unnecessarily. You should try returning to the present. Even though it may be challenging to accomplish most times, you should not worry.

Case studies

Mindfulness practice is an art that deals with alertness and focusing on every detail by individuals. If you apply mindfulness appropriately, it breeds reliability for the organizational procedures. But then, no study can measure the cost of integrating mindfulness which seems vital for managers who wants to allocate their scarce means amongst the competing enhancement initiatives.

Another case study from Australia Research about Mindful Meditation by Dr. Stacey Waters explores the present mindfulness practice in the Australian schools. The study centers towards executing mindfulness programs in the schools throughout Western Australia. This innovative research involves various curriculum-based cases inside the schools that are popular for implementing mindfulness strategies or programs.

These case studies involved focus groups and interviews with the main stakeholders and students in every school. The evidence that backs the implementation, planning and evaluation of these strategies and programs were also gathered, and evaluated. The objective for each of the school-based study is to create a holistic concept of the workings of a mindfulness program in every school.

According to a case study from CVS group which is the biggest veterinary group in the United Kingdom, mindfulness approach is founded on acquiring gained delivery. The first case study in the mindfulness initiative's presentation, states that the suicide rate in the veterinary field is almost twice the rate in the medical and dental professions. According to the study, the issues of well-being and stress have the same importance as radiation, fire or other hazards. As a result of this concept, the CVS Group decided to offer their entire staff mindfulness training. During the case study, the significant decreases in the staff stress levels were measured statistically. After the exercise, the report shows an improvement in the staff resilience after six weeks mindfulness training which is carried out for 20 minutes each day.

There is a staff member that was suffering from depression all her adult life who joined in the mindfulness training. According to her testimonial, the mindfulness training helped her where psychiatry and tablets had failed. Now, she is confident to participate in meetings and dares to bring out her ideas.

A case study from a workshop by Dr. Brandon Nappi who is the Executive director and founder of Copper Beach Institute states that the mindfulness is a science that focuses on the present without passing judgment. According to this case study, about 1,000,000,000 heartbeats are the longest lifespan for every living thing. This means that we should try to enjoy each one of the heartbeats. Another case study states that up to 2,000,000 American citizens practice mindfulness.

A mindfulness study carried out on 15,000 workers from Aetna group shows that on the average level, about 28% of the employees' stress levels were reduced. There is also a 20% increase in the sleep quality level while 19% for pain reduction. The report shows that after this mindfulness training, the employees have become highly effective in performing their tasks. This training increased their productivity by 62 minutes each week which brings the Aetna's worth to $3,000 per year for every employee.

## Chapter 9: Mindfulness & Meditation

Mindfulness & Meditation
Meditation plays a crucial role in attaining mindfulness. I used to look down on meditation. I didn't understand the appeal and thought it was pointless. Why I felt this way, I don't know. I had to wrap my head around meditation when I decided to give being mindful a try.

It took time, but I came to realize the positive impact meditation could have on me. After only a few months of practicing, I was pleased with the difference I saw in how I used to view the world compared to how I currently viewed not only the world but myself as a person. I now practice meditation every morning and take walking meditations during my day. I hope you'll be able to discover some of the benefits I did from embracing meditation.

Meditation is great for managing stress and easing the pressure we often place on ourselves. Meditation teaches you how to keep your mind still and focused. It teaches you how to quiet the noise in your mind and shut off the self-monologue that often plays in your head and messes with your ability to achieve inner peace.

Practicing a mindfulness meditation each day will train your mind to find appreciation, calm, love, and happiness in your daily lives. It will give you the tools needed to push past any obstacles standing in your way and it will teach you a sense of well-being and purpose. You need to learn breath control and mindfulness to unlock the power of meditation. Once I mastered both skills I could become more mindful of my thoughts and actions.

People often believe when you meditate you're trying to let your mind rest in peace by stopping every thought. People new to meditation often feel like they're doing things wrong because they can't turn off all their thoughts. However, this is an incorrect meaning of meditation. When you meditate you're supposed to have thoughts. Mindfulness meditation is what we do with thoughts as they occur. When you feel distracted by thoughts, you'll want to bring your attention back to whatever the object of your meditation is. That's the way you'll learn to relate differently to future distractions. As time goes on, it will improve your ability to concentrate and remain focused.

Meditation has different forms. You should contact a local group or teacher to guide you while you're first beginning. You can often find resources at yoga studios, local gyms, senior centers, and places of worship. Many doctors will also be able to give you references. I took the recommendation of a friend when first starting out.

Mindfulness Meditation Instruction

Here are simple instructions on how to get started with mindfulness meditation. Use the form of meditation you desire but this is my favorite and the one I practice daily.

1. Get a chair or cushion to sit on. Keep your spine straight. Relax slowly into a comfortable sitting posture. Take a few calming and deep breaths. Allow your mind and body to relax. Make sure your mind remains attentive and alert. Make a note of body parts that feel tense and parts that feel relaxed. Don't try to fix anything. Go with the flow.

2. Allow your mind to remain soft. Allow awareness to wash over your body. Feel the sensation of sitting. Use your mind to get past any tendencies you have to think about your body. Thoughts and images should come and go as they please without feeling concerned or bothered by them.

3. Feel all of your body and any awareness that comes from within you, but not from your mind. Being aware of your body will anchor you and keep your attention focused on the present moment.

4. Sweep all of that awareness throughout the rest of your body. Feel every

sensation. Don't attach agendas or goals just focus on the moment. Be mindful of each new sensations and remain in the moment.

5. Once some time has passed, you can move your awareness to any sounds around you. Being aware of sound will allow you to create receptivity, openness, and spaciousness in your mind. Remain aware of both the sounds and the silence occurring in-between sounds. As with the sensations of your body, you'll want to shift awareness away from trying to define any sounds or having thoughts regarding any sounds. Only hear the sound as it is.

6. After time has passed, bring your full attention back to your breathing. Locate your breath where it's clearest and keep your awareness there. For example, the rising and falling of your chest.

7. When you breathe, let your breath go without controlling it. Feel the breath from within only the breath itself, not from the

head. The aim is to feel the full cycle of your breath from beginning to the end.

8. Let go of everything around you. Allow it all to rest in the background. Your breathing should remain natural without you trying to force it. The goal is to rest in a deep state of relaxation, remaining mindful of your surroundings and your breathing.

9. When your mind wanders, be aware of it and guide your mind back to your anchor without passing judgment. After you've practiced this it will become second nature. It's hard not to judge oneself. Over time you'll learn how to stop.

10. Remain in the moment, staying mindful of your surroundings for as long as possible. Focus on every breath, remaining anchored. Work at this. Over time you'll extend the length of time you can meditate for.

11. The more you meditate, the more you'll remove unneeded attachments and

fears. It will let you live a happier life, filled with compassion and wisdom.

## Chapter 10: Mindfulness And The Present Moment

If we were to look truthfully and honestly at the way you spend your time, we would notice that we are always in an autopilot mode. We are planning for the future. We are looking at the past and wishing we did things differently. We are always completing to-do lists and worrying about the next item on that list.

We are so caught with moving forward into the future that we have no idea how to enjoy the present moment. Eckhart Tolle says this of most people, "They are looking at the present moment like an obstacle which needs to be overcome so that they can reach the future." "This attitude is insane," he says, "because the present moment is nothing but life and with this insane attitude, these people are not really living."

Look at the following instances in your life: Being excited about traveling somewhere, reaching the destination, but completely forgetting the journey

Waiting in anticipation for a great dinner experience and afterward not remembering anything you ate or tasted

It is possible that the above instances have taken place many times in your life and you don't even realize what you have missed, isn't it? It is all because our minds were lost in some thoughts somewhere else other than the present moment.

Yes, our days are more or less made up of mundane activities including cleaning, eating, driving, doing dishes, etc. Yet, these are the chores and work activities that make up our lives and there must be some way to live mindfully from moment to moment completely engaged in each of our little activities, no matter how seemingly boring or mundane they are.

Practicing mindfulness is the most efficient way of leading a fulfilled and happy life filled with wisdom involving the awareness from moment to moment of everything that is taking place within and outside of us. From within, we become more aware of our mind, thoughts, and body while from the outside, we broaden our vision and see everything that is happening around us making us more alert, still, and yet content.

Do a little exercise right now. Take your eyes off of this book and look around you. What do you see? If you are in a room, notice the size of the room. Is it big or small? If you are outside, can you see the enormity of the sky above you? What are the sounds you hear? Notice and observe. See if you can identify the sounds and sights. What about smells? Can you identify any smell or is the surrounding completely odor-free?

Now, turn your focus to your body. Can you sense anything? Can you feel the pressure of your buttocks on the seat? Does any other part of your body feel stressed out? Is there a sense of discomfort or comfort in your present arrangement? What is your mental state? Are you happy, sad, or depressed? Don't be judgmental. Simply watch, observe, and notice everything as acutely as possible. Let your mind behave like a curious child who simply wants to know and not pass any kind of judgment to his or her learning. The child is happy if you answer his or her questions. Feel the amazement of doing this for the first time like how a child would feel if he or she had chocolate for the first time. Feel the wonder of the things within and around you. This is the beginning of becoming mindful and being in the present moment.

Masters and practitioners of mindfulness will tell you that being mindful and being in the present moment helps you lead a peaceful and stress-free life as you slow down to enjoy every passing moment in its entirety. Moreover, practicing mindfulness helps you be more joyful and happier than before.

Without mindfulness in play, our minds are dulled into a monotony of uncontrollable and wavering thoughts. These thoughts not only create stress but also have the power to take away our ability to absorb a part of the abundance of joy available in the present moment. These thoughts of the past and/or of the future have robbed us of our natural curiosity and the joy of discovery. We are so caught up in the inner voices and thoughts that we fail to notice the abundance of joy in and around us that is there for ours to take.

As we practice the art of mindfulness, we become more aware of everything and notice even the small things that we have either taken for granted or forgotten it exists. Take the mindful breathing exercise, for example. We have taken for granted our ability to breathe. We have forgotten the immense power of this breath and how without it, we can be dead. The deliberate attempt to focus on the way the air inhaled and exhaled; the way our body behaves as we breathe, etc. are meant to draw the attention of the amazing mechanism on which our life hangs!

We are, in truth, surrounded by an abundance of happiness and beauty. It is possible to eat, walk, and live each day mindfully so that we are constantly in touch with this plentiful source of happiness and joy that surrounds us. Thich Nhat Hanh, a Buddhist teacher and proponent of mindful living, makes a very illuminating statement in this regard.

He says, "We are very good at preparing to live well. We are very good at working hard to earn money so that we can buy that coveted car, house, etc. We are ready to work hard for 10 years to get that diploma which will give us a higher salary than now. However, we forget that are alive right now and at this moment, which is the only moment there is to be alive." He further adds, "Every moment we live, every breath we take, every morsel of food we eat, everything sight we see, every emotion we feel, can bring serenity and peace for us. We simply need to be present in the present moment to partake of the joy."

Mindfulness and Difficult Times

The practice of mindfulness is not an exercise in achieving bliss throughout your life. It is an exercise to help you handle difficult and troubling times too. Mindfulness is all about being attentive without being judgmental; observant without arriving at any 'right' or 'wrong' kind of conclusion about anything or anybody. Mindfulness teaches us to notice and watch everything without wishing things were different irrespective of whether the situation is good or bad.

In a negative situation, our emotions are so powerful that we are easily led astray with non-productive thoughts that don't help us in looking at anything in a positive light. It is so easy at such times to think and react based on negative thoughts impulsively and do things that we might regret later.

By practicing mindfulness, we actually put a safe distance between ourselves and our emotions giving us the needed insight to look at them objectively. This will help us release the sense of attachment we have towards our emotions. So, our outlook from 'my anger' changes to 'being angry.' It changes from "I am very angry," to "I am in a temporary state of anger which will soon pass away."

Practicing mindfulness is the most effective way of being in the present moment. Mindfulness allows your mind to be broad and expansive allowing you the freedom to fit in all kinds of perspectives without judging them in any way. It empowers you to look at everything objectively so that solutions for problems are easily visible.

## Chapter 11: Learning To Meditate

Meditation is a crucial mindfulness practice that everyone should invest in. Meditation is the art of truly letting go, quieting your mind, and connecting with yourself in an intimate way that embodies full awareness and consciousness. This practice can be as simple as you make it, and is a great way to begin truly embodying mindfulness in your life. In this chapter, we are going to explore a practical and effective way to implement mindfulness into your daily life through meditation. This will allow you to build your practice and truly become self-aware and mindful on a greater level.

If You're New to Meditation

If you have not already established a meditation practice in your life, you may be curious as to how you can powerfully implement meditation. Meditation is a great mindfulness practice, and it can be extremely easy to begin meditating on a regular basis. The key is learning to work **with** your mind.

Meditation is a practice that we must establish and grow on our own terms. Like other skills, some people will pick it up and do phenomenally right away, and others will have to take their time and build their skill. This is not something that you can compare with others or compete with others on. Instead, it is something that you have to build within yourself. When it comes to meditation, some days it will be easy and others it will not. Typically, on the days when it is not easy, you can confirm that those will be the days when you need it the most. On the days when it is easy, practice anyway.

When you are beginning your meditation practice, start with something small and simple. For example, the mindful breathing practice from Chapter 4. As it becomes easier for you to stay focused on that minute of breathing, expand your practice to last for two minutes. Then, grow it to three minutes, and four minutes, and eventually five minutes. Each time it gets easier, add another minute. Once you can comfortably meditate for about 10 minutes, you are well on your way. While you can certainly meditate for longer, ten minute meditations are long enough to provide you with all of the benefits of meditation. They are also short enough that they can easily be integrated into your daily routine.

As you are meditating, you want to do your best to draw your awareness to your body and stay focused on your physical self. Notice your breath and any areas of your body where you may be feeling various sensations. It is completely natural for your thoughts to stray, even when you have a regular meditation practice. Do not punish yourself for straying. Instead, once you become aware that your thoughts are astray, you can draw them back to your body. You may have to do this several times in a single practice, or you may only do it a few times. There is no right or wrong number. The key is that you release judgment and allow yourself to come back when the time feels right.

Expanding Your Practice

As meditation becomes easier for you, you can begin to expand your practice. Ideally, you want to continue having meditations solely devoted to becoming aware of your body and tuning into yourself. However, you can also begin implementing meditations that have a specific intention. The most common intention is to tune into something that may be bothering you, such as stress or frustration, and finding out "why?" As you begin to develop answers, you can then use these answers to eliminate the stress or frustration from your life.

The best way to determine what type of meditation you need is to ask yourself. Consider how you have been feeling recently and take a few moments to notice whether or not there is any particular emotion or feeling that seems to be taking away from your peace and happiness. If there is not, you can engage in a regular meditation. If there is, you can set the intention that your meditation will focus on that particular feeling or emotion. The guided meditation below is a great meditation to use in either situation.

Remember, each day that you meditate you are going to feel differently. Some days it may come easy, and other days it may not. The key Is to focus on what you need at the moment. Release judgment and expectations and simply use this as a time to tune into your body and needs and give yourself the mindful attention is required at that moment. If you would like, you can keep a mindfulness meditation journal that will allow you to track your journey. This can be a great help in becoming aware of what truly helps you when it comes to releasing stress and frustrations and drawing yourself back to a state of peace.

A Guided Meditation for Mindfulness

The following guided meditation is a great meditation practice that you can follow when it comes to establishing a mindfulness practice. This meditation is one that will allow you to focus on mindfulness as a whole, or on specific elements of your emotional body if required. It is great for sending healing and peace to dis-eased emotions or energies within your body, or simply tuning in and sending peace to yourself as a whole. Read through the meditation and then use it as a guide for your next meditation practice.

"As you begin to sink into your meditative state, begin to draw your awareness to your feet. See if you can notice any physical sensations on your feet that draw your attention in. Are they comfortable? What does the temperature of the air feel like against them? Are there any other physical sensations you notice against or within your feet? Draw your awareness then up to your ankles, taking notice of the same sensations, or any new ones that may appear. Then, draw that awareness up through your shins and calves. As you begin to take notice of each new sensation and feeling, spend a few moments with it. Does it feel good? If the answer is no, ask yourself why. See if you can uncover the ailment that is bringing discomfort to this space. Consciously note any ailments that may come up and set the intention to bring healing to them, both now through your awareness, and in your daily life. Draw your attention up through your knees, and into your thighs. As you continue to meditate and scan your body for sensations, focus on your glutes, your pelvis, and your hips, now. Then, draw your awareness up into your lower abdomen and back. As you continue, draw this awareness up your spine and through your torso, then into your chest and shoulder blades. Continue asking yourself how each sensation feels, and if it is a positive or a negative feeling. Express gratitude for your positive feelings, and set the intention to bring healing to your negative feelings. Draw the awareness up through your neck, then up into the back of your scalp. Draw it over your scalp like a hood, noticing the top of your head. Then, draw it down to your forehead and your eyes. Lastly, bring your awareness to your face, including your cheeks, jaw, lips, tongue, and nose. After you have completed scanning your body, you can allow yourself to naturally come back out of your meditative state and resume your daily activities."

By doing a full body scan like this, you allow yourself to draw awareness into all areas of your body. This is a great way to check in and learn to move your awareness around and set the intention of truly becoming aware of your entire physical self. It is also a wonderful opportunity to take note of any areas that may not be feeling stellar and truly bring awareness to them. This is your chance to stop ignoring your body and its needs and to begin serving it in a greater way, through self-awareness and mindfulness. When your body brings an ailment to your awareness, take the time to intentionally cure that ailment. This will allow you to take your mindfulness to the next step and truly honor everything your body and mind share with you, rather than ignoring anything that they bring to your awareness. Ignoring these sensations and signs will only further support a lack of mindfulness as you essentially train yourself to ignore your body and mind's pleas for assistance or attention.

## Chapter 12: Building Your Self-Confidence

As mentioned in the previous chapter, self-confidence is a direct product of a positive self-esteem. This too, can be developed or built. People like to be around other people who are brimming with confidence. Confidence is the belief on your ability to do things, to act in a specific way, to play a role, and other similar things. Make no mistake about it, but you can overdo the building and use of confidence. This is known as arrogance.

Of course, you will learn the thin line that separates arrogance and confidence when you work towards developing your self-confidence. Are you now interested to know how you can build your self-confidence? The pieces of advice you might get will vary depending on whomyou willask for help. However, the best and simplest ones are enumerated below:

**Look good to feel good**: This might sound generic, but it actually works. Take a look at the way you dress up. Do you fit in with use of "smart dressing"? Of course, you have to also work on your fitness level. A good level of health and fitness also leads to a good level of self-esteem and of course, confidence.

**Teach your body to show signals of confidence.** Yes, people can sense confidence through the body language you are showing. These signals are as follows:

Erect body posture – This reflects smartness, alertness and dominance.

Right amount of relaxation – Even though you are standing erect, you should make sure that your body is not stiff or rigid.

Walk quickly and without hesitation – This signifies that you know what you will do next.

Heads up - Holding your head up conveys the message that you are indeed confident about your abilities and whole self.

Always smile – The power of smile has always led people to positive circumstances. Have you ever heard of the line "smile and the whole world smiles back at you"? Actually this is true. Smile and get your confidence level up.

Make eye contact when you talk with people – Through this, you are giving the sign that you really mean and believe what you are saying. It will also assure another individual that you are honest and sincere.

**Use the 3P technique of self-affirmation**: Get yourself energized by saying positive, personal, and present tensed daily affirmations. Don't include negative words in your daily affirmations, always refer to yourself, and speak in such a manner as if you are already in possession of what you are saying.

**Set goals but make these realistic**: This way, you have a good chance of attaining each goal. You will feel good about yourself every time a goal is achieved and this leads to an increased level of self-confidence.

**Build and maintain healthy relationships:** These relationships should be built on mutual trust and friendship. Give and take compliments graciously. Honesty, love, kindness the desire to bring out the good in others, and the readiness to forgive should be in these relationships. The more meaningful relationships you build, the more that you will see your confidence level growing.

**Love yourself:** This may sound too vague, but it really implies simple things that you can do. Look within you and accept your abilities and imperfections. Have the desire to solve your imperfections or weaknesses. If you have passions, you must pursue these individually.

Building your confidence is very much possible. Follow the things mentioned above. Do it with consistency and determination to succeed. You'll see the results sooner than you will expect.

## Chapter 13: Mindfulness Exercises For Stress, Pain And Success

Mindfulness is known to be the best way to release the stress that builds up during your day. Mindfulness meditation does help with stress, but stressful life usually doesn't give you the opportunity to take some time to release your stress and this even makes you even more stressful.

Even though stress can be very bad for your life and your health it is also playing a necessary part in life. Because stress brings learning, creativity, and your survival and it becomes harmful when it is overwhelming and can interrupt your nervous system and that is why it needs to stay balanced. Unfortunately, too much stress now is common in this contemporary life.

Thankfully mindful relaxation techniques can bring the balance of your nervous system. This relaxation exercise is done by producing a relaxation response with the state of calmness.

When your stress is overwhelming, your body starts to fill up with chemicals that will prepare you for a "flight or fight". Stress response is lifesaving when it comes to emergency situations and you need to act quickly. But when you do that, your body wears off, especially when the stress response is active every day. With the mindful stress relaxation exercise you will be putting a break and it brings the mind and body into a balanced state.

How to produce the relaxation response

There are many different mindful relaxation exercises that will help in bringing the nervous system in balance and one of them is the meditation that you already read about. However, there is one exercise that you can use it depending of your busy life.

So, this stress relief mindful exercise is based on creating relaxation response and it is not about sitting down and lying on the couch or even sleeping. It is mental active process and it will leave your body calm, focused and relaxed.

To learn the basic relaxation exercise is not difficult, but still it needs practice, like everything else in life. It is recommended to take 10-20 minutes free time in your day to do the practice. If you have time and you want to relax even more, do it for 30 minutes or even an hour. If you think that this is a very daunting commitment for you remember that this exercise can be placed into your daily schedule without changing it, during your lunch, at work or in your morning routine.

Find the best relaxation exercise for you

The key to finding the best relaxation exercise just for you is by choosing one that can be incorporated into your daily life routine. When you are choosing the right exercise for you consider all specific needs that you have, like work, housework, fitness, meetings and other preferences. The best exercise is the one that will fit into your lifestyle and resonates with you. You have to be able to focus the mind without interruption of your thought so that you can awake the relaxation response. There are cases when you find that combining and altering different exercises can keep your motivation up and it will bring you the best results.

To choose the best way to exercise is by finding out how you respond to the stress. This has an influence to choosing the relaxation exercise.

- "Fight" Response: If you become keyed up, agitated or angry when you are under stress then your response to the stress has to be by exercises like meditation, muscle relaxation, guided imagery or deep breathing. This means exercise that will calm you down is the best for you.

- "Flight" Response: Becoming spaced, withdrawn or depressed when you are under stress then you have to do stress relief exercises that will energize and stimulate the nervous system like massage, power yoga, or rhythmic exercise.

- Immobilization response: If you experience a type of trauma or you tend to "stuck" or "freeze" when you are stressed then the best exercise for you is to do physical mindful activities that engages both the legs and arms, like dancing or running.

The three different exercises for different type of stress reactions might seem different, but they are not. This is because they hold on something same, mindfulness. Remember to always be mindful, aware of the exercises. Be aware of every step you take when you run or dance. Be aware of the environment and your thoughts. When you get the massage done be aware of how it relieves your stress and your breathing pattern and also how the muscle relaxation affects your body.

Mindful Exercises for Pain Relief

Mindfulness provides an accurate view of pain. For example, you are thinking that your pain is there all day, but when you bring awareness to the pain it will reveal the actual peak of the pain. You think that your pain is there all day, but when you are aware of it you will see that your pain is there just a few times a day.

If you are struggling with any type of pain, even a chronic one, mindfulness exercises are the best way to approach the pain.

Body Scan

With body scan you will bring awareness to each part of your body. You will bring attention from what your brain wants to step away from. Instead of reacting to your pain immediately, the body scan will teach you what the brain is experiencing.

Breathing

As you can see breathing is almost never excluded from mindful exercise. It is an essential part for almost all types of mindful exercises and also for this one. When your pain arises, your brain will react automatically. Even though you are not able to completely stop the pain you will be able to lower the negative thoughts and to calm the mind and to "ground the breath".

Simple as the breathing, when you are practicing mindful meditation, take a breath in and out, be aware of the breath how it travels in your body. Then you can ask yourself what is the important part to pay attention to.

Distractions

Distraction and mind wandering can be a very helpful tool when the pain is getting worse, anything that is above 8-10 scale. The key is to find a healthy and mindful distraction. For example, it can be something like focusing on conversations with friends, cooking, reading an interesting book or something you find very distracting.

Mindfulness is the best practice to approach any kind of pain. It will teach you to observe your pain, and to become curious. This act, to pay attention to the pain is what will help you.

## Mindfulness for increasing success

Becoming mindful won't just help you in dealing with negative emotions and thoughts, but also it will help you in increasing your success in life. There are few mindful exercises that can help you with that.

When you understand how mindfulness works and the concept of it everything will be easier. Also, when you get around mindful meditation and it is already your habit, you can get even deeper into mindfulness. Every time you practice it you get better at it and you can add more exercises that you can do anytime and anywhere. Same goes for the next exercises for success.

## Notice, create and seek out new things

One of the most necessary mindful exercises for success is to notice, create and seek out new things. The important key is to notice and also bring into your focus new things for the present situation. This includes people, work and environment. When you are committed to notice the new things in your life you will be more creative and you will develop different and new solutions to your problems. You will see more than one option and you will eliminate the defined past solutions that now will no longer be of use because the situation is different.

The result – There will be less frustration, higher sense of achievements, improved outcomes and increased confidence.

Understanding the behaviors differently in different situations

As a mindful person you will recognize the deeds and the words, someone else's or your own, will make sense in given context and in what way they are delivered. For instance, when the action you have taken hasn't turned out as planned and ended in failure, it is important to remember that the decision you have made in that given moment actually made sense, but only at that time from your point of view in the given context. It is not good to judge yourself for the action. You did the best you could in that context and with the information that was given to you.

So, next time when a person did something that made you angry or embarrassed try this: think about at least 3 positive reasons why that person has acted in that way. Why did it make sense to him/her and not to you? What is his perspective?

The result is – more understanding, open to see the situation in a positive way, lower stress, and stronger relationships with friends, colleagues and family and greater empathy.

Transform your mistakes into success

When you try to transform something you see as a "failure" into a fresh idea, you are using the mistake to create another application so that you can get a positive outcome.

When you increase the perspective it will result in higher creativity and also innovation. Then ask yourself how that "failure" can be your way to get a new and fresh idea to have a successful outcome in your business and work. Almost everyone only focuses on a single outcome of the work and so we create a process, which we think, will increase the possibility to achieve the outcome. When that objective is not met we make a mistake of throwing away everything and just focus on overcoming those "errors".

The best approach is to be more aware and to see new creative approach and to examine the process and to find three new aspects that will be beneficial and also three outcomes that you haven't planned about.

Be aware of all the emotion

When you understand that your emotions are the result of your perspective and mindset then you can be in control of the reactions in you. Things are not negative or positive; we make them by our judgments and thoughts. On the other hand, with mindfulness you will be open to see more ways to look into situations and you will find opportunities that were hidden from you. This process will put you in control and you will be stressed less.

Authenticity

When you are untrue about yourself and to yourself, your life won't work positively. To be authentic means you can question the wisdom of what doesn't work and what does, what is not allowed and what is. Remember that those that are making the rules are people and those rules aren't immutable. There are many ways to do one thing. When you act in a mindful way you will remain true to yourself and to your own values. You will be happier, engaged, and successful in your life, work and relationships and make them even more meaningful.

Following these simple steps your life will turn another way, a successful way. You will be successful in different aspect of your life and not just in your work. Your relationships will get better and you will be more connected with people, your work will shine and you will be happier.

How to go to bed mindfully

Sleep is one of the most important parts of your daily life. This is because when you sleep you don't just get energized but also feel rested for the next day. Sleeping is also essential for people who are practicing mindfulness. You can't go to sleep not being mindful when you have practiced mindfulness the whole day. Plus, the additional benefits that you will get form going to bed mindfully are huge.

Going to bed mindfully you will sleep better and deeper. Especially for those who cannot get sleep fast and or for those who may have a disturbed sleeping pattern or for those suffering from insomnia.

When you go to sleep you are letting go of everything in the world, it isn't something that you do, and it is about doing nothing. In this kind of sense, sleep is a lot similar to being mindful. When you give your best to fall asleep you are putting too much effort and most of the time it gives the opposite result.

Here are few tips and exercises, that can prepare yourself to go to sleep in a mindful way and this is the way all mindful people are doing it.

1. First of all, remember to go to bed every day at the same time and also wake up at the same time. To wake up one day very early and the next to sleep more will confuse the body clock and it can cause problems to fall asleep.

2. Don't bet yourself to be on your phone, computer or TV before you go to bed. Turn off all electronics for at least 30 minutes before you go to bed.

3. Get few minutes before your go to bed to practice a mindfulness exercise. It can be anything that we have already

discussed, body scan, breathing, meditation or other thing that suits you.

4. Try to do some gentle stretch or yoga. Naturally, cats stretch before they curl up to take a nap or to sleep. This kind of a stretch will help you relax your muscles especially if you have had a very hard working day.

5. You can take a mindful walk indoors and not just outside. Take 5 or 10 minutes and walk and feel the sensations that are in your body.

6. When you are already in bed, feel your inhalation and exhalation, don't try to sleep just be there with your breath. Start counting your breaths 1 to 10 every time you release your breath. When your mind begins to wander, start again from the beginning.

7. If you are worried about something, accept your worries, make sure you note them, and then you can get back to your breathing.

If you are having trouble falling asleep more than usual, do not put your mind into it. People have different sleep cycles and most of them have bad nights too. If you can't fall asleep it doesn't mean that there is something wrong with you. Your sleep will get better every time you do the mindful practice before you go to bed.

**Chapter 14: Letting Go**

Letting go is a very important part of meditation. It's also a very important part of life. In the earlier chapters, I showed you how to clear your mind, but you need to be able to do this on a regular basis so that it becomes a habit. When bad things are said or there is the likelihood of an element of regret, it leaves traces in the mind that the emotions can pick up on at any time of weakness. That's almost like building up barriers within your mind that stop you from being able to grow spiritually.

Learn not to take offense

Do you remember what you are supposed to do with thoughts when you meditate? The idea is to let go. When someone says something that would normally leave you feeling angry, replace anger with empathy. Think that the comment comes from someone who is lacking in discretion and should therefore be let go of. It's not important enough to poison your mind with anger. I found one of the easiest ways to deal with this is simply to agree. People don't expect that and it kind of makes them think twice before they say something of this nature again. You can't be held responsible for the words of others. What you can do is simply let them bounce off you and not let them penetrate your otherwise peaceful mind.

Know when to walk away

Walking away is a useful way to catch your breath and to calm your mind. Walking meditation is used to help you to clear your mind of something that has upset you. Instead of concentrating on that one thought and making it larger, you simply concentrate on the movement of your feet and breathe in the same way as you do when you are meditating. A few moments of walking meditation can clear all of the cobwebs of conversations that may otherwise have led to misunderstandings and being exaggerated out of all proportions. Dismiss yourself politely and simply walk.

Learn to listen

Sometimes we just get snatches of conversation and don't recognize when friends actually need us to listen. If you have the slightest clue that someone needs you, arrange a time when you won't be interrupted so that you can give that friend all of your attention. Listening is a powerful part of using the senses that you were given and can cement friendships and really help you to empathize. Don't interrupt. Let your friend talk and actively listen.

Learn to laugh

When was the last time that you were able to laugh with all of your might and feel it right down to your tummy? Laughter is release but it has to be appropriate and it has to be something that gives you back that inner child. In my case, I have YouTube videos that I find very funny indeed. The fun isn't mean. It's just so laughter inducing that I use it when I feel stressful. Let yourself laugh. Your soul needs it and when you do laugh, don't hold back. When you laugh wholeheartedly, you let go of so many stresses inside.

Let go of self-doubt

This is a huge stumbling block for a lot of people. They try to take on too much and get overwhelmed. If you find yourself in this predicament, break down what you have to do into manageable proportions and just do one small task at a time. For example, if you know you need to clean the house, choose one closet to start with. If you know you have to clear all the paperwork on your desk, sort it into manageable proportions and then tackle each of them one at a time. Self-doubt comes when you are overwhelmed but if you become mindful of this feeling of being overwhelmed, you can diminish it by making things more manageable.

Celebrate Life!

Every day I wake up, I am grateful for everything that happens within the course of a day even if some people see part of that day as negative. If you change your viewpoint, and see every element of your day as being necessary to make your life whole, you learn to accept the bad with the good and see both of these as being elements that keep you on your toes and alive. If you find yourself flagging during the day, open up the journal that you wrote earlier and look at all the things you chose to be grateful for at the beginning of the day. These are valuable. At the time you open up the journal, you will probably find you have dozens more things you could add to your gratitude list. Life is a celebration and staying within this moment, try to see all of the opportunities rather than holding onto the negativities. Let go of them.

Let go of worry

Let's take a look at what worry is. It is thoughts about an event that has not yet happened. Thus, it's hypothetical. If you allow your mind to be ruled by the hypothetical, you need to remind yourself of ridiculous hypotheticals that didn't happen to see how pointless the exercise of worry is. For example, the world didn't end in 1981 as predicted. The car didn't get stolen overnight as you thought it may have done because you left the keys in it. The bathroom didn't flood even though your daughter insisted on running a deeper bath than you thought was necessary. Stop worrying about moments in your life that have not yet arrived. If you find yourself doing this, step back into the moment you are in because this is the moment you should be enjoying. People who worry don't actually realize much of the time how much discomfort they place on people around them. My mother in law is a typical example. She worries all of the time about things that are unimportant and consequently makes us dread her vacations spent with us because we know they will be fraught with worry. Let it go and live in the moment.

Let go of obligations placed on others

You are only responsible for your own life. You can't control the lives of others and when you try to, often you have to deal with disappointment because your priorities may not be theirs. It's okay to forget sometimes. It's okay to be so busy in your life that you forget obligations to others, but when you don't place people under an obligation, you don't have to deal with the consequences of being let down. Stop expecting others to have the same priorities as you. If they do something nice for you, then be happy. If they don't find the time, then be happy too because by imposing things on others, we are putting out own expectations in life onto the shoulders of minds over which we have no control. When people do nice things for you – appreciate everything that they do. That way, you control your own level of happiness and anything anyone else adds to it is seen as a positive thing.

## Chapter 15: Mindfulness At Work

If asked what the most stressful part of their day is, a vast majority of the population would answer the workday without hesitation and with good reason. The combination of increased responsibility coupled with a lack of control combines to form a perfect storm that naturally leads to high levels of stress, anxiety and tension, often without any relief in sight. Luckily, mindfulness meditation, when practiced discreetly, can not only help mitigate these symptoms, it can also make it easier to focus on a particularly arduous task or project, often leading to unexpected insight and outside of the box thinking. As an added bonus, the state of calm that practicing mindfulness provides, not to mention the boost it will provide to your ability to empathize with others, will surely help to make you extremely popular around the office.

While not possible with all professions, with practice you will find that you can squeeze in a few minutes of mindfulness meditation here and there throughout the day. While the individual efficacy of any particular mindfulness meditation session might be relatively minimal, the overall gestalt will lead to a sense of wellbeing that is greater than the sum of its overall parts. While it might seem difficult to deal with the demands of the day, the demands of your coworkers and everything else that life throws at you, you can consider each micro mindfulness meditation session as islands of calm in an otherwise choppy sea. Mindfulness in the workplace should be thought of as a tool that allows you to squeeze every bit of efficiency out of the workday as long as you think carefully about how to use it as effectively as possible.

If you have already used the period of time prior to arriving at work as an opportunity to practice mindfulness meditation then when you arrive at work you will ideally already be in a state that is primed for making the most of every moment. You can then keep the mindfulness mindset rolling by taking a minute or two between tasks to focus on your breathing and the sensory information that your body is providing you. This doesn't need to be an elaborate process, it can be as quick and as simple as it needs to be. Remember, in this instance quantity definitely trumps quality. Make a point of practicing every day, but if you miss a day, don't use it as an excuse to form unproductive habits, simply pick up where you left off and start again.

Many people find that clearing their minds at work can be exceedingly difficult. If your job leaves you precious little time to sneak in a little mindfulness meditation then your best bet is going to be to start slowly with as little as thirty seconds of mindfulness meditation at a time. With practice, you will be able to sneak in a little mindfulness more frequently until you are ultimately able to string a whole day's worth of micro meditations together with ease.

Types of micro meditation

For those with office jobs, one of the easiest ways to practice mindfulness meditation at work is by focusing on the sensations that your fingers provide you as you your hands move across the keyboard. Note the rhythmic sound of the keys being pressed and pay special attention to the feeling of your fingers pressing down on each individual key. Consider carefully how your mind forms each word prior to your fingers making it a reality and spend some extra time thinking about the connection between mind and body that is taking place as well as how it is so often taken for granted.

If you find yourself sitting for most of the day, prior to starting your micro-meditation it is important to consider your posture. Start by relaxing your entire body starting with your neck and working your way down to your toes before reversing the process and starting at the bottom and working your way up. Once you are relaxed focus on the signals that your body is sending you in an effort to pinpoint any areas that are crying out to you in pain. With the problem points identified you are then going to want to adjust your posture until you are completely pain free.

If you spend a majority of your day responding to emails or various phone notifications then you can simply add thirty seconds between each reply to center yourself and practice mindfulness in its most minute form. While thirty seconds here or there isn't going to do very much good all on its own, the cumulative effect will surprise you. For example, if you respond to eighty requests requiring your response per day then you are actually spending forty minutes of your day being mindful. Give it a try and you will soon realize just how effective this practice can be if you keep it up.

If your job requires rote repetition then any time you are performing a mundane task you will find that it is an excellent opportunity to practice being mindful. Any activity that mixes physical activity with an ability to only focus on the specifics of what you are doing in a passive way is essentially a free pass to be mindful. All you need to do is focus entirely on the current task and you will be able to easily fill your day with mindful thoughts.

If your job requires you to constantly interact with coworkers then you can practice mindfulness by simply devoting all of your mental energy to listening to what the other person has to say. While you might not always appreciate your coworkers' insights, giving them the full scope of your attention will allow you to find a state of mindfulness while at the same time allowing them to feel as though you really care about whatever it is that they are saying.

Additionally, this is a good opportunity to practice improving your overall level of empathy as you can use each conversation as an opportunity to try to determine the other person's mindset in an effort to empathize with their position. Remember, the goal here is to focus on the conversation you are having to such an extent that everything else leaves your mind, you won't be able to multitask but others are sure to see your interpersonal skills go through the roof. During these conversations, you are going to want to give some thought to your body language as well, avoid crossing your arms to ensure you appear open to what the other person has to say. You will also want to consider the amount of space between you and the other party as you don't want to interpose any objects between you nor do you want to end the conversation at a distance that is much greater than where you started.

In order to maximize the effectiveness of your end of the day commute and the mindfulness meditation you are hopefully practicing therein, you should use the last few minutes of the workday to compartmentalize everything that has happened during the time you were hard at work. Consider what you have managed to accomplish, reflect on your successes and your failures in light of the bigger picture and consider what they mean overall for the days to come. With that done, mentally close the door on the workday and remind yourself that any work problems won't need to be solved until tomorrow. Close the book on the workday before you leave your place of business and you will find your next session of mindfulness meditation to be much more effective than it otherwise might be. Above all, repeat the mantra that tomorrow is another day and another opportunity to get everything right.

While it might seem that making an effort to practice mindfulness in the office will lead to an overall decrease in productivity, the reality is that the opposite is true. Especially if you have a particularly hectic job you likely find that you often have to react to things without thinking through all the possible outcomes of your response. With your head cleared from frequent micro-meditations, however, you will find that the moments in which you have to make important decisions naturally seem to expand in order to provide you with all the time you need to make the right choice, right now.

Remember, when you react to something you at taking a nearly automatic action, letting the stimuli that sent you down this path take control of the situation. However, if you respond instead of react then you are making a well-reasoned choice based on all available data. Reasoned responses lead to better solutions every single time.

With enough time spent practicing mindfulness at work, you will also find that you have gained the ability to approach problems both old and new in ways that you had previously never considered. This will only be the case, however, if you stop thinking about incidents that require your attention as problems and instead consider them in the framework of challenges to be overcome. Problems are simply roadblocks to success while challenges, on the other hand, are incidents that can be learned from and bested for the betterment of you and your place of business. When you come across a challenge that has you stumped, consider writing it down and focusing on it completely to the exclusion of everything else. If you have been practicing mindfulness regularly you will be surprised at how quickly a previously unthought of solution may reveal itself.

## Chapter 16: Mindfulness To Eliminate Stress

Many people are not going to like what this chapter has to say, but if you really want to eliminate stress from your life using mindfulness you need to consider what is being said.

First, I want to address the fact that yes, mindfulness does involve accepting the situations in your life and knowing that there really is not anything you can do to change the situation. However, that does not mean we have to accept situations we can change.

You need to be mindful of all of the situations that are causing you stress in your life that can be changed. For example, you can make a list being honest about the situations in your life that are causing you stress. Once you have the list you need to consider the things that can be changed.

One situation in my life that was causing me a huge amount of stress was my job. Yes, I was able to get through each day by practicing mindfulness, however I was not happy with accepting the situation. I was working 7 days a week, 12 hour days, never seeing my children. When I picked my children up at night, I fed them dinner, bathed them and put them to bed.

No matter how much I practiced the method of being mindful, I knew something had to change. Now I still work 12 hour days, 7 days a week, but I do it from home. My children are not being raised by a babysitter, they are at home, being taught the things I want them to learn and being raised the way I want them to be.

Now, I am not going to say that this change did not cause some stress in my life. It did cause some anxiety when I first began working at home, but by using the process of mindfulness I was able to overcome that stress and anxiety.

Just because you practice mindfulness does not mean that you cannot change the situations that are causing stress in your life. I want to make sure you understand this completely. I don't want you to think that just because you practice mindfulness you have to accept everything as it is and never make any changes for the better.

If that were the case, I would still be working away from how 12 hours per day, 7 days each week and my kids would still be spending the majority of their life in someone else's care.

## Chapter 17: Increase Your Chances Of Success

This chapter serves only one purpose. It's to suggest that a healthy life is not strictly about meditation and mindfulness. It's like jogging to get more fit, but having a cigarette when you finish. Bad example, but I think you get the point.

So, here is a bullet point list of my do's and don'ts to reap the benefit of yours and your kid's mindfulness practice.

Do's:

Eat as much unprocessed food as you can afford. Normally, you find all this good stuff on the outside isles of your grocery store.

Make sure your kid gets ample sleep. In most cases, 8 or 9 hours isn't enough.

Let your kids fight, argue, and generally get into trouble. But...always make them accountable for their actions and don't let them get away with shit!

Model your behavior. Act like the adults you want them to be.

Play games with your kids (especially games outdoors). Families that play together, stay together.

Don'ts

Reduce or eliminate screen time. It's a brain killer - the research shows that your kids brain physically changes for the worse the more time they spend watching a screen (any screen).

Don't let your kids be lazy. Chores, homework, sports, part time jobs, volunteering. My wife is a high school teacher. Without a doubt, kids from farms where they have a lot of chores make the best students. Hard work and a can-do attitude are the best attributes for scholastic success.

Don't accept poor manners. A child won't go far in life if they can't treat people nicely and respectfully.

Don't be friends with your kids (at least until they've reached their twenties). Your kids need to know that your relationship is parent/child and the boundaries this implies. It certainly doesn't mean you can't be friendly and spend time together having fun, but your kid always needs to be reminded that how they treat their friends is not how they treat you.

This isn't the most comprehensive list of do's and don'ts, nor do I offer evidence that these principles are well-founded. However, from my experience and those that I work with, if you adopt some or all of these ideas, if you haven't already, you will find that your mindfulness sessions with your kids will be more meaningful and effective.

**Chapter 18: This Is Your Brain On Stress**

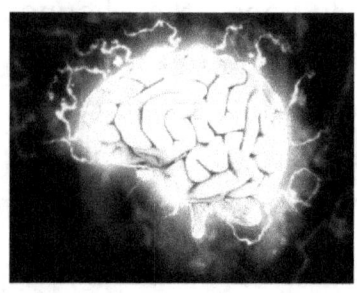

To understand why mindfulness is the antidote for negative emotions causing stress, you first need to know something about your mind and how it works. The human brain has evolved over time, and the way it has evolved can tell us a lot about why stress is so harmful.

A Brief History of the Brain

If you are like most people, you think of your brain as a single organ. Although that perception is true to a point, it is also a bit misleading. The human brain has distinct areas that function in different ways. One explanation of those functions refers to the brain as being triune, meaning that it is composed of three parts.

1. The basal ganglia, also known as the Reptilian Brain, is the most primitive part of your brain, and is the home of the "fight or flight" response. This response is at the heart of your body's response to danger. Your Reptilian Brain is active when fear is present and takes precedence over everything else in your body. It calls all of the shots, and until its fears are assuaged, it will be very difficult for your brain to learn, think, or function in a rational way.

2. The middle, or Mammalian Brain, is driven by emotion. It is more evolved than the Reptilian Brain, but still not capable of logic. It can be easily distracted by negative emotions.

3. The neocortex, also known as the New Brain, is the most highly evolved part of the brain and is responsible for your ability to rationalize and apply logic to situations. This part of the brain can function properly

only when the basal ganglia and middle brains are calm and satisfied.

## The Fight-or-Flight Response and How It Hijacks Our Lives

Now that you understand the basic structure of the triune brain, let's go into some more detail about the fight-or-flight response and what it does to you when you experience it.

The fight-or-flight response is a defense system in your body. When you encounter a situation that threatens your life or safety, it triggers a particular biochemical response that helps your body prepare to do one of two things:

1. Battle the danger (Fight); or
2. Run from the danger (Flight.)

What does that mean in biological terms? First, it means that your body releases two important hormones, adrenaline and cortisol. You are probably familiar with the effects of adrenaline. It increases the flow of oxygen to your muscles, and it makes you feel wide awake. Your heartbeat speeds up, as does your breathing. It takes energy away from certain bodily functions, such as digestion, and makes the energy available to you so you can use it for other things, such as running. It sharpens your senses and can even make it seem as though time is slowing down.

Cortisol, also known as the stress hormone, prevents inflammation and increases your blood sugar so that you have energy available if you need it.

Short, infrequent episodes of adrenaline and cortisol release may be useful. However, if you spend a lot of time in this state, these chemicals can have harmful effects on your mental and physical well-being.

The problem with the way your fight-or-flight system works is that your body cannot tell the difference between a perceived danger, such as an impending deadline or a stressful phone call, and a situation that is truly a matter of life and death. Biologically, your response is the same when you get an angry email from a client as it would be if you came face to face with a lion.

It is easy to see why this response can be a problem. An email is not a lion, and reacting as if it were one is unnecessary and unproductive. When your fight-or-flight system is activated, it is very difficult to engage in rational thought. Your Reptilian Brain is running the show. That means that your New Brain, the part of your brain that you need to work effectively or help your kids with their homework, is out of commission.

## What Stress Does to Your Body

The effects of stress on the human body are well documented, but many people do not realize how harmful it can be. Chronic stress can have a dire impact on your physical and mental health.

Your body experiences stress when the fight-or-flight response is triggered. It doesn't matter whether the catalyst for the response is spotting a bear when you're out for your daily run or getting a reprimand from your boss. You know now that biochemically speaking, the response is the same. Your body is full of adrenaline and cortisol. You feel anxious and jittery. Concentration is impossible.

When your body experiences stress on an ongoing basis, this is what can happen to it:

■ Your blood pressure can increase, which, over time, increases the chances that you will experience a heart attack or stroke.

■ Your stomach churns and you may experience nausea or diarrhea. Serotonin, an important neurotransmitter, is found in both the brain and the stomach. Its presence is the reason stomach issues often accompany stress.

■ Your blood sugar increases and your resistance to insulin decreases, which can, over time, lead to hyperglycemia or diabetes.

■ You lose bone and muscle mass. Cortisol steals glycogen (stored glucose) from muscle as it would if you were starving. It can also weaken your bones.

- Your immune system is weakened. Cortisol can help reduce inflammation, which is a good thing if you are injured. However, in the long-term, you need your immune system to keep you safe.

The presence of adrenaline and cortisol in your system is a good thing when you run into a tiger and need to react quickly, and a very dangerous thing when your brain thinks you might run into a tiger all the time. You can see how important this brain function would have been for our caveman ancestors, but tigers and those types of threats really aren't issues anymore, so this brain function is now a hindrance.

Because your body cannot tell the difference between a stressful situation that requires the release of adrenaline and cortisol and one that does not, the only way to manage your stress is to learn how to cope with it and calm your mind when you need to do so. That is where mindfulness comes in, and that is what we will talk about next.

### Chapter 19: Mindfulness Thinking

It has been said that as a man thinks, so he becomes. It has also been said that we can transform ourselves when we renew our minds. Despite that, many people tend to underestimate the power of their minds. Probably it's because people usually think about comic book heroes with uncanny telepathic towers that can move or even destroy people and things simply by thinking so. But believe it or not, our thoughts can be just as powerful in how it can affect our lives for the better or worse.

If you want to change your thinking patterns from one that's depressed, anxious and stressed, meditation is one of the most powerful methods available to you. Basically, meditation is all about training your mind or achieving a particular level of consciousness that will allow you to experience several benefits that include among others mental vitality, relaxation and confidence, which are the opposites of depression, stress, and anxiety, respectively. Other benefits associated with meditation are:

More stable emotions;

Increased creativity;

Better intuition;

Significantly clearer mind;

Ability to manage or address problems much better;

Sharper mind; and

Wider consciousness.

Now, let's look at 3 very good exercises that you can perform to help you practice mindfulness in your thoughts. Apart from helping you develop mindfulness and win the war against depression, anxiety and stress, these your schedule can easily accommodate these exercises so that you won't have any reason not to perform them.

MINDFULNESS THINKING EXERCISE: OBSERVATION

To begin this exercise, get any object or item that's easily within reach. Anything will do – ordinary or special doesn't matter. The important thing is you pick up something. If you're a housewife, you can consider picking up a kitchen item or a figurine adorning your home. If you're a businessperson, you can consider picking up a booklet of unissued receipts or one of the items you're selling in your store. If you're a student, you may consider grabbing your ID or a notebook. Again, the object isn't relevant – the important thing is you pick up something for use in this exercise.

Now that you have an object, do the following:

Hold the object with your hands, right in front of you.

Focus your entire attention on that which you're holding and allow yourself to be completely engrossed by it. Try to observe the object at a level of detail you've never done before. If you're holding a piece of orange for example, try focusing on the ridges on its skin. Keep in mind that you should avoid studying, judging, assessing or evaluating that object – just notice or observe the object's nuances and details.

While you're doing this, you'll start to experience how it is to be in the so-called "moment" – also referred to as being in the present. You will also observe that as you continue practicing this, your mind will be able to more and more easily release any thoughts you wish to let go of.

It will also be able to experience the pleasures of simply being in the moment – in the present.

This exercise may be very subtle but make no mistake about it – it's a very powerful mindfulness meditation exercise! It may seem to ordinary and that nothing's happening immediately but if you commit to practicing this daily for at least 2 weeks, you will start to notice its beneficial effects.

## Chapter 20: 30 Simple Mindful Techniques You Can Practice Anytime

We can learn and practice mindfulness without forcing ourselves to sit or stand in any specific, complicated postures in stillness for long periods… These are simple ones. They are so down-to-earth that it will be love at first sight!

1. Conscious Breathing

"Feelings come and go like clouds in a windy sky. Conscious breathing is my anchor." - Thich Nhat Hanh

How many of us do that? We breathe, but do we know when our breath deepens or turns shallow? Are we aware of the pace of our breath? Well, most of us just take breathing for granted. After all, it is just air passing in and out of our lungs, right? But let's now change the concept… Let us try breathing consciously!

Sit, stand or lie down. Just choose a posture in which you are most comfortable.

Close your eyes and relax your body.

Take a deep, long whisk of air in through your nose.

Feel the way it fills your nostrils and moves deeply into your lungs, expanding your chest and abdomen.

Exhale the air through your nose, keeping your mouth closed. Keep the exhalation long, preferably longer than your inhalation.

Repeat 4 more times.

Now resume your normal breathing and observe the sensations and difference. Something different... something beautiful just happened, right? You can keep count, say 5 for your inhalations and 10 for your exhalations... 5 to 7 rounds are normally sufficient to relax your mind and bring your focus back.

Caution: Do not try to judge the quality of your breath; just keep counting...

2. Conscious talking

Let's try to be conscious about what we talk about... We don't do that regularly and consistently! Spend a few minutes a day talking with awareness. Try not to judge the words... try not to criticize the choice of words. Just be aware of the way the words flow... the tone and pitching.

3. Conscious posture

Do we notice the way we sit on our chair while working, or the way we sleep? Well, I generally don't! The result – I find myself waking up with a sore and nagging back! It's pretty natural... So, the next time we sit, let us try sitting upright, keeping the spine straight and aligned with our neck and back. Our backs will thank us! Bonus – we fill find it easier to finish our work, as the right posture improves focus and concentration by instilling a new sense of mindfulness in our body and mind.

4. Walking in nature

"Walk as if you are kissing the Earth with your feet," says Thich Nhat Hanh in his book Peace Is Every Step: The Path of Mindfulness in Everyday Life.

And, unarguably, it is one of the most effective and simple techniques that help us establish that self-awareness. Spending time in nature is healing. And when we do that barefoot, it allows us to connect with Mother Earth and ground, which in turn helps us to remain mindful. You can do this in your lawn or a nearby park. Or just take a walk near a flowing river under the full lit moon... It's just awesome!

Remove your sandals/chappals/shoes.

Feel the rustic ground beneath your feet.

Walk slowly and as you walk, place your feet in such a way that the soles are in complete contact with Mother Earth.

Imagine that your feet are hugging Her and bestowing Her with love and kisses.

Spend about 2 to 3 minutes... And then, put your shoes on and start walking... You will feel the difference!

5. Mindful brushing

There are several things that we do so often that we almost don't notice them anymore. Brushing our teeth is one such activity that we perform on autopilot mode... Our mind starts wandering, worrying about our daily plans, meetings and the date we have after 3 or 4 days, and what not!

Tomorrow morning just try to focus and experience it. Try to feel the way your tooth brush moves over your teeth. Feel the taste of the toothpaste. Finally, when you rinse, feel the cool water fill and cleanse your mouth and teeth, leaving you refreshed and awakened! Fabulous!

6. Drinking tea/coffee

This is yet another thing we just do in a hurry. We neither savor its aroma nor its taste. We just gulp it down and rush. But the next time you want to drink a cup of tea or coffee, just try to bring in a small sense of awareness. Right from the moment you brew, consciously add the tea or coffee... savor the aroma the drink leaves as you pour the boiling water into it. Swirl in the sugar/honey and notice the gentle 'whirlpools' the spoon creates... Finally, when you sip it, just cherish the aroma and flavor... You will find yourself in a different world!

7. Taking a soak/shower

This is my favorite morning mindfulness exercise. I spend a good deal of time under my shower! Just give yourself a good, gentle massage, from head to toe. Now, stand under the warm shower and feel the droplets of water falling on your body, cleansing and nourishing your body and soul. As you lather in your favorite shower gel, inhale its aroma. Let the gentle fragrances calm, soothe and revive your senses. Wash off the excess soap in the shower and dab dry with a soft cloth... Have you ever taken a shower like this before? How are your energy levels now?

8. Mandala coloring

We all used to love coloring as kids. Mandala coloring is for the kids that sleep deep within us adults. There are numerous patterns available and you can take a printout or get a book from your nearby bookstore or from online stores. Use crayons, pencils, or water color and just get started. Awaken your Inner Child; do not judge or be bothered about the choice of colors. You just have to make sure that you are coloring without trespassing the borders. Careful coloring connects us with our true self and with regular practice, it alleviates stress, helps us stay calm, and in turn, boosts mindfulness.

9. Eating mindfully

You can practice mindfulness while you eat. When you take the first bite of any meal, just take a moment to really pay attention to the color, texture, appearance, feel and taste of the food. Use all your five senses. Look at the food carefully, feel the textures in your mouth, enjoy its aroma, and notice how your body reacts to it. You don't need to keep this up all the way through the meal, but use it every now and then to focus your attention.

## 10. Being self-compassionate

Self-compassion is essential to develop compassion and sympathy for our fellow beings, but how often are we self-compassionate? Don't we often indulge in self-abuse, showering ourselves with words of scorning, judgment and harsh criticisms? Let's now spend 5 minutes a day being mindfully self-compassionate! It would not only uplift our moods and revive our day, but it also gives us a new sense of happiness, joy and confidence that will change our lives forever.

## 11. Remaining calm throughout the day

Try not to lose your temper, whatever happens. Just for one day – or say, for a couple of hours. It's okay if your dishwasher stops functioning. It's okay if your cranky boss is yelling. It's okay if your child is screaming. Just try to remain calm and silent... This mindfulness calmness is, in fact, a big stepping stone to developing a sense of relaxation.

## 12. Give and expect nothing in return

Have you ever practiced this? We always expect something in return for whatever we do. When we complete a work before time, we expect a surprise bonus. When we work overtime, we expect additional pay. When we give someone something, we expect a return gift. Why don't we spend a day giving anything and everything without expecting anything in return? Try it!

## 13. One minute gratitude

Practicing gratitude is a good habit. It multiplies our blessings, makes us happier and leads us to fulfillment and contentment. We do say 'Thank you" but do we express our gratitude for all that we have, every single moment, every single day? Well, most of us do not. Just spend one minute expressing gratitude right from your heart to anyone and everyone, anything and everything!

14. Be assertive mindfully

Most of us are scared of saying no. We love to be people pleasers. But just try to be assertive and say no in a mindful way, without judging yourself. Just do that to your overbearing boss or pestering friend! You will experience an immediate shift in your energy levels!

15. Conscious thanking

This is an extension of technique 13. Practice gratitude every night before you hit your bed, irrespective of how your day went. Mindfully include all the aspects – small or big – and thank. The next morning, repeat your gratitude exercise. Begin with a big, wholesome thanks to Almighty, God, Higher Self – whatever name you give that supernatural power – and go on with the list you left behind the previous night! Your day will be fab!

16. Celebrating small successes

We all celebrate, but only if the successes are really tangible. We mindfully become mindless about all those small, small things that we achieve daily. Let's now change our way. Let's try to celebrate our tiny wins as well. The next time you experiment with a recipe in your kitchen or just fix a bug in your program or write a blog post, just give yourself a pat on your back and say "Yes, I did it." But don't do it for the sake of doing it. Congratulate yourself mindfully, whole-heartedly and then, just pay attention to your body's sensations!

17. Honoring your commitments

We do keep our appointments; we do meet our friends. However, how many times have we pressured ourselves to ensure that we do not fail them? How many times have we met others with that sober expression and done things as if we are doing it just for namesake? It's time to revamp... Take a deep breath and mindfully acknowledge the commitment. Thank the person consciously in your mind, smile to yourself and then go ahead! You will feel the energy shifting!

18. Surrendering your obsessions

Many of us are obsessed with something or other. It could be the way things are arranged in your home or the place where you practice yoga in your studio. We start frowning and making faces even when the slightest changes happen. The next time such a subtle change occurs, just take a conscious deep breath for a count of 4 and just say "I surrender my obsession. It is okay for me to let go of it." Repeat it a couple of times... You are bound to feel better.

19. Facing your fears

Facing our fears is frightening. I remember reading somewhere that fears are nothing but "False Evidences Appearing Real." They are not true; they are our illusions, trying to scare us, pushing us away from our path. Whenever I feel some fear creeping up inside me, I just accept the fear. Accepting and acknowledging that the fear is coming will help us face them and release them. Once we accept them, just tell them "I don't need you. You are just an illusion. I now release fear and choose love over fear." Make sure you keep breathing. Just repeat this for about 5 to 9 times to feel grounded!

20. Letting people rant

People rant and keep ranting for some or other reason. Let's now mindfully let them rant without getting bound to their energies and issues. We are not the reason for their ranting. So, the next time someone comes up with a complaint, just listen and let go. Remember, no judgments, no criticisms!

21. Facing gossip with silence

Someone has rightly said that silence is golden. When we choose to face the gossips without reactions, we choose to become mindful. We ensure that we are not affected by any such negative talks. We can either walk away with an assertive statement or just let the person finish his/her gossip and then politely say "Thank you", and then move to the next task without thinking, reviewing or judging the scenario and the person.

## 22. Staying non-judgmental

It is a key element of mindfulness. When we choose to remain non-judgmental about the past or future, we choose to live in the present. When we choose to remain non-judgmental about a person and his deeds/words/actions, we choose to accept and acknowledge ourselves as is. When we are non-judgmental, we are mindful! Just try doing it in each and every simple thing you do. Remember, there is nothing like the right or wrong way of doing things. It is just what we think!

## 23. Making jewelry

Crystals are wonderful healers. When you befriend them, they reciprocate their love. Making jewelry and mindfulness are connected… Right from the moment you choose the crystals or beads, the supplies and other things required for making the bracelet/necklace/earring, we establish a connection with them. We do things so mindfully that it becomes like a mindfulness meditation. Try using an amethyst or crystal quartz to make your favorite jewelry as they are known to help in inculcating mindfulness!

24. Playing with clay

Shaping the clay is an art... a mindful art! The slightest mistake can spoil the complete efforts! Be it the water we add or the heat of the furnace, one has to be pretty careful. Even if it is the Play Doh that our kids use, we need to be extra conscious while molding them into what we design...A tweak here or there could be disastrous! It is time for us to revisit our childhood, right?

25. Stop the victim attitude

We do not have to play the victim attitude when we are experiencing some really crucial situations. We do not have to play the role of the helpless. Instead, choose to accept and acknowledge the situation.

Being consciously aware will help us find a solution.

## 26. Enjoying a foot soak

How many of us have actually experienced the sensations flowing through our body and feet as we soak our feet in lukewarm water filled with salts and essential oils? Well, if you haven't done that before, try it today! Fill your tub with lukewarm water and add a cup full of Epsom Salt/Himalayan Pink Salt. Add a couple of drops of essential oil of your choice. Now using your hands, stir the water to release the aroma. Inhale the scents and feel the way they refresh your mind. Gently soak your feet. Close your eyes and feel the sensations. If your mind wanders, bring it back to the way the water soothes your tiring feet.

## 27. Cleaning our bowels

We often sit in the restroom for minutes with newspapers, books or mobiles as we clean our bowels. But since our health starts at the gut, keeping it healthy is very essential. Do not let your mind travel into the day's tasks. Bring it back mindfully.

## 28. Fasting

Fasting is not just good for our body; it is good for our mind as well. But we often try to keep ourselves busy while we fast, so that we do not fall prey to the lust called food. Let's now do it a little differently. The next time you undertake a fast, just observe the way your body reacts. When you feel hungry, listen to the signals your body gives you. Are you comfortable with the process or are you just doing it because someone else said it's good? When hunger strikes, make a conscious effort to sip lukewarm water and now notice the difference. Take mindful naps while still being aware of the reactions. As you end the fast, notice how your body reacts. Mindful fasting is more beneficial than mindless ones.

## 29. Playing crosswords/puzzles

It is a pretty simple way of cultivating mindfulness. Sudoku, in fact, is the best mindfulness challenge game...a number missed here or there can fail you! Try playing the game for a while to unwind, de-stress and become mindful!

30. Playing memory games

As kids we used to play memory games... It was either pairing up the same cards by keeping them upside down or just observing an array of things and writing them down on a piece of paper later, without seeing them... Conscious observation is what helped us here. Let's repeat that again. Try playing such games with your kids or create ones of your own choice. There are memory games online as well!

These 30 techniques are pretty simple, but if you want to remain mindful every given moment, they are not sufficient. That is why I have elaborated on a couple of mindfulness meditation techniques which you can practice daily!

Are you ready?

# Chapter 21: Applying Mindfulness Meditation Daily

Mindfulness meditation involves the art of tuning in to your senses while remaining in the present moment. Fortunately, you can apply mindfulness into your daily life. Most people think that mindfulness meditation is merely a practice that involves emptying the mind of unnecessary thoughts. While part of it is true, mindfulness meditation is about focusing one's attention and training the mind to become more focused, skillful, and efficient in daily life. You can integrate mindfulness meditation into your daily activities by tuning into your senses, helping you to be in the present moment instead of getting lost in thinking. There are several steps that you can follow to integrate mindfulness meditation into your everyday life.

Being mindful in conversation involves listening as a form of meditation. Make sure to pay attention to the person speaking. Notice the sound as well as the rhythm of their voice. Observe their facial expressions. During conversation, you might notice your mind wandering off or thinking while the other person is talking. Take note if it is easier for you to talk or to listen. Observe if there is an urge to speak.

You can also apply mindfulness meditation when you eat, when you are in grocery queues, or when on social media. As discussed in the previous chapters, you can practice mindful eating by taking note of the taste, colors, smells, and shapes of the food on your plate. Focus on the sensation of chewing as well as the texture, flavors, and temperatures inside your mouth. Observe if there is an urge to swallow food without chewing or eat quickly. Take note if your mind wanders off and gently bring back your focus on the food.

If you are in a grocery queue, instead of getting irritated or impatient, focus your mind on your feet touching the ground or the sounds that you hear. Try to tune in to your body. If you notice a feeling of impatience or irritation in your body, avoid clinging to it and focus on your breath.

Prior to checking your accounts in social media, make sure to consciously plan the amount of time you intend to spend. Take note of the urge to keep checking through the feeds. Notice if any emotion arises as you experience the lives of other people in your social media.

## Conclusion

Hopefully, you now have a better understanding of how meditation can benefit you. From reading this guide, you will have gained a deeper understanding of how your mind works and how meditation alters your brain to work at its optimum. From producing the hormones and chemicals, we need to live without stress, anxiety, or depression. To be happy and balanced in our thoughts and actions.

The true test, of course, is to try it out for yourself. By this I mean really try it. Give yourself a window of time each day that you safeguard for meditation. Although it is far easier for a beginner to do this somewhere quiet and without disturbance, it will eventually be possible for you to practice meditation almost anywhere.

Make it part of your daily life, like eating, drinking, or brushing your teeth – you do brush your teeth, right? If you can make meditation habitual, then you will reap the benefits for the rest of your life.

Don't be shy about it either, spread the word, tell your friends just how awesome it is and help change someone else's life too.

www.ingramcontent.com/pod-product-compliance
Lightning Source LLC
Chambersburg PA
CBHW072011070526
44583CB00015B/1430